TO HARRY BICKFORD
   A FRIEND, FELLOW
GARDENER AND FELLOW
BRIDGE PLAYER.

          Gene Luce
          1-11-92

Tango *under way off Columbia River, May 3, 1942.*

Tango Around the Horn

The World War II Voyage of America's Last Large Sailing Ship

Revised and Expanded Edition

by Lawrence Barber

Oregon Maritime Center and Museum
Portland, Oregon

Tango around the Horn: the World War II voyage of America's last large sailing ship.

Revised and expanded edition. $13.95 Softcover.

Publisher's Cataloging-in-Publication Data

Barber, Lawrence, 1901-
    Tango around the Horn : the World War II voyage of America's last large sailing ship / by Lawrence Barber. ---Rev. and expanded --- Portland, Or. : Oregon Maritime Center and Museum, c1991.
        p. : ill. ; cm.
    Based in part on the log of Archie McPhee and the diary of Fred Bitte, with a chapter by Gene Luce.
    Includes glossary and index.
    ISBN: 1-880827-01-8

    1. Tango (Schooner) 2. Sailing ships—History—20th century. 3. Merchant seamen----United States—Biography. 4. World War, 1939-1945—Personal narratives, American. I. McPhee, Archie. II. Bitte, Fred. III. Title.

HE745.B   387.5'0973 dc20

Published by Oregon Maritime Center and Museum, 113 S.W. Front Ave., Portland, Oregon 97204

Printed by Maverick Publications, Inc., P.O. Box 5007, Bend, Oregon 97708. Printed in U.S.A.

Dedicated to the memory
of
Archie McPhee, ablebodied seaman
and
Fred Bitte, carpenter-donkeyman
on *Tango*'s last voyage around the Horn.
They inspired this report.

ABOUT THE COVER

This portrayal of the *Tango* rounding Cape Horn is a watercolor by
William T. C. Stevens, a marine artist of Portland, Ore., for 30 years. He
depicted the big vessel with a port list as a result of the shifting of the
lumber deck load and only four of the ten sails up. Two of the sails later
were dropped to ease steering in the heavy seas. Cape Horn is shown
hazily over the stern.

Artist Stevens came by his profession fittingly by serving three years
of the Korean War as Lieutenant on an American destroyer. He has been
a small boat sailor for 30 years and is a member of the Portland Yacht
Club. A graduate of the University of Washington and the Northwest
College of Fine Arts, he is a signature member of the American Society
of Marine Artists.

IN APPRECIATION

This publication by the Oregon Maritime Center and Museum was
made possible by financial contributions to the Center's TANGO Fund by
the following friends, relatives, and associates of the author and the center:

William F. White, Margaret Ann White Rothman and Donna Broun-
stein, in memory of the late Thomas Jefferson White; Mrs. Archibald D.
McPhee and Colleen McPhee, of Beaverton, Ore.; Kathleen McPhee
Zaleski, Fairfax Station, Va.; Linda McPhee, Newport, Ore.; Shirley
McPhee Pearson, Milwaukie, Ore.; Lisa McPhee Leask, Patricia F.
McPhee, Jessica McPhee Hays and Karen E. McPhee, all of Portland,
Ore., in memory of the late Archibald D. McPhee; Miriam Bitte for
Margaret T. Bitte and family, in memory of the late Fred Bitte; the late
Frederic DeLos Barber, Longmont, Colo.; Ralph F. Barber, Provo, Utah;
L. Eugene Barber and Lawrence F. Barber, Portland; Ruth I. Brandt and
Austin Leach, Portland; J. Richard Nokes, Portland; Margaret Ware,
Honolulu; Helen Rose, Pomona, Ca., and others.

Table of Contents

Appendices

List of Illustrations

What It's All About

July 1, 1943

"We are really in it now—60-foot-high waves and an 80-knot wind. The only sail we had to put up was the staysail, and the wind got it about 11 a.m. The steam pipes on deck are all torn up. The puddin spar for the starboard lifeboat was broken. Six barrels got adrift on deck, but the sea was so heavy we could not lash them down; so we just cut holes in them, and when they emptied the sea took them overboard. The Captain has finally decided we couldn't make it to Santos and now wants to head back to Durban. To protect himself, he wants all of us to sign the log that we think the ship unseaworthy for the trip. We agree to this, for the rigging is all going haywire and the canvas is rotten because the sails were not taken care of properly in port. The ship has an exceptionally fine hull and really rides heavy seas nicely. Everybody is disgusted and fed up with the ship and dirty weather. This is the worst weather most of the fellows have ever seen. I got some good pictures of the storm. In one hour after I wrote that last bit at 6:55 p.m. a 10-foot sea broke over the poop from the rear. Pearce and Lindbergh were on the wheel. The sea knocked Pearce right through the wheel, breaking out a third of it, and it is a sturdy, brass-bound, hardwood wheel. It threw Lindbergh right over the rail and into the rigging. He was lucky he wasn't tossed overboard. Pearce was unconscious for a half hour and is in the hospital with chest and back injuries. This same sea went right through into the galley, flooded out the stove and took everything off the table and shelves, and half-drowned the cook. The seas and wind reached their worst about 8 p.m. and the sea must have been about 80 feet high. the only thing we could do was to run with the sea or get battered to pieces. We figured we were traveling about 8 knots without a sail up. It was in a southeast direction, just the opposite of where we want to go."

*   *   *   *

The foregoing is a crew member's vivid report of one wild and stormy day and night in the career of America's largest sailing ship in World War II. The vessel was the 360-foot six-masted bald-headed schooner, *Tango*, which successfully sailed from the Columbia River around Cape Horn to South Africa during the early days of the war, when Axis submarines and surface raiders were roving the seas to intercept and sink defenseless Allied merchant ships.

The *Tango* and its crew of 17 adventurous men was lucky. It survived fierce storms and mountainous seas, and avoided enemy fighting ships, to finally deliver its cargo of lumber in Durban for use in the mines. It then loaded a cargo of coal for a daring voyage across the South Atlantic to Santos, Brazil, a trip thwarted only by 80-mile winds that ripped its sails to shreds and by 80-foot seas that threatened to destroy the sturdy vessel.

Tango was 38 years old when she made that long wartime voyage around the Horn. She was the last large U.S.-flag commercial sailing ship to make that passage.

She was not always American, nor was she always a schooner. She was built in 1904 in Glasgow, Scotland, as a four-masted bark for German owners who gave her the name *Hans*. The finest of her kind, she was employed in the coal and nitrate trade between Europe and the west coast of South America until the outbreak of World War I, when she was interned at Santa Rosalia, Mexico, with other German ships.

In the years between the two big world wars, she came into American ownership and two name changes. After more years of idleness at Oakland, California, she was purchased by Las Vegas gamblers who had her towering masts, rig and deckhouse stripped away and converted her into a gambling barge to be anchored three miles at sea from Long Beach harbor.

Put out of business by California authorities, she was laid up again until World War II created a market for old hulks that could be rerigged as sailing cargo carriers. She was the last and largest of these vessels, and was refitted as a six-masted schooner to haul lumber to South Africa. She retained her gambling name.

This book tells *Tango*'s story, high-lighted by the "log" of her final days under the U.S. flag as it was kept from day to day by Ablebodied Seaman Archibald D. McPhee and the diary of Fred Bitte, the ship's carpenter-donkeyman on the last long voyage.

McPhee and Bitte, both of whom signed-on at Portland, Oregon, with the other 15 men, told how the pick-up crew members got along, their fun, poor food, personal fights when tempers strained—and much, much wild water and fierce winds.

The early chapters are based on the personal knowledge and research of two previous authors, J. Ferrell Colton, who had a part in the restoration and rigging of *Tango* and told about it in his book, *Windjammers Significant* (J. F. Colton & Co., 1952), and Captain Harold D. Huycke, whose volume, *To Santa Rosalia, Further and Back* (Mariners Museum, Newport News, Va., 1970) fills in details about the German crews stranded in Mexico during the first world war. Both were seamen as well as writers. They gave their blessings for use of information on the construction, operations and early history of the vessel contained in their splendid publications, now out of print.

The author of this account was a newspaperman covering the *Tango*'s rigging and loading at St. Helens, Oregon, and her departure from the Columbia River in May, 1942. Bits and pieces were taken from my articles published in the

Portland *Oregonian* after U.S. Navy censors released the stories long after the ship was out of sight.

Valuable assistance and criticism was received from John C. Capell, Captain Eugene Harrower (USNR-Retired), and others. Artist John Blasen drew the sketches of the *Hans* and *Tango* sails plans.

The author believes the *Tango*'s story is closely typical of other large working sailing vessels of the time when steam was displacing wind-power and motorships were replacing steamships. *Tango* was one of the last of an era.

Archie McPhee and Fred Bitte were both retired in Portland, Oregon, when they inspired this work and supplied their log, diary, and some pictures, as well as advice and assistance until the late spring of 1987. Then, to our great sorrow and dismay, both suddenly passed on to that new world where good sailors go. Archie died of a prolonged respiratory problem, April 26, at a time when we expected his expertise in wrapping up details. One month later, May 25, Fred passed away in his sleep. He had been fading away for several months.

With them gone, only one member of the original crew was believed left and he had "disappeared". After the original printing of this book appeared on the market, the "missing" radio operator, Gene Luce, surfaced in retirement at Seagrove, North Carolina. His uncle and cousin in Oregon learned of the book and purchased copies, sending one to Luce. They notified the author of his whereabouts, and the new chapter 16 resulted.

We welcomed Gene Luce's reminiscences and reflections.

Lawrence Barber
Portland, Oregon

Chapter 1

The Handsome *Hans*

The owners of the stately new four-masted bark *Hans* were justly proud of their handsome vessel when she was launched in April, 1904, in Port Glasgow, Scotland.

She had the finest hull lines a naval architect could devise and her masts reached 198 feet from keel to truck.

She was one of the largest sailing vessels in the world, 360 feet long, and with few exceptions she had about the largest cargo capacity of any. She was a true bulk carrier.

Beside her was her identical twin sister, *Kurt*, being made ready for launching a few weeks later. The twin sisters were named after two sons of Edmund Siemers, head of the leading commission house of G. J. H. Siemers & Co., of Hamburg, Germany.

Siemers & Company was founded in 1811 by George J. H. Siemers and became a major firm engaged in hauling and selling heavy bulk commodities between Europe and the western coast of the Americas. The company owned a fleet of ships, steamers for carrying high-grade packaged goods, sailing vessels for the bulky fuels, fertilizers, grains and lumber, and petroleum tankers. *Hans* and *Kurt* were designed and built to be the finest in their class of all in the world.

Generations of Siemers followed George in operating the business, and in 1903 Edmund J. H. Siemers, a grandson of the founder, decided the firm needed a pair of very large, well-found sailing vessels, the finest money could buy, to head the fleet hauling coal, coke and briquets from Germany and Wales to Chile and Mexico to fuel the furnaces of copper smelters and bring back nitrates, grain or lumber.

Siemers was in competition with other German, French, British and Scandinavian firms operating fleets of bulk carriers in the same trade.

A contract for construction of the new vessels was let in 1903 to the prestigious shipbuilding firm of William Hamilton & Co., Ltd., Glasgow, and work began immediately. Both ships were to be four-masted barks of the highest classification by Germanischer Lloyd, the German counterpart of Lloyd's of London.

They were to be identical in dimensions and fittings. The waterline length of each was 335.5 feet, extreme width 46.9 feet and depth of holds 26.5 feet. Following their launchings, measurements determined that Hans was of 3102 gross registered tons and 2880 net tons, while Kurt was slightly greater, 3116 gross tons and 2911 net tons.

Siemers & Co. estimated the deadweight capacities of both vessels were 5393 tons. Both later carried cargoes of 5,000 to 5,500 long tons.

The hulls were declared to be exceptionally fine. One expert who saw *Hans* on drydock declared she was "like an ocean liner." Years later, when she was under the American flag and named *Tango* and on a Los Angeles drydock, she "was the talk of the waterfront," according to historian J. Ferrell Colton.

Hans and *Kurt* were known as "three island" vessels, a popular deck arrangement at the turn of the century. The islands consisted of the forecastle, an amidship house, and the poop. Both vessels had four hatches.

Masts, spars and bowsprits were heavy steel tubes. The fore, main, and mizzen masts stood 198 feet from keel to truck, and each was assembled in two sections. The jigger mast was 153 feet 6 inches, keel to truck, and in one piece. Yards were steel tubes about two feet in diameter at their centers and tapered outward. The royals measured 48 feet long, while the lower spars were 91 feet long. The bowsprit was a 64-foot steel tube, two feet six inches in diameter, and tapered forward.

Both ships carried full suits of 35 sails, 18 of them "square" and 17 fore-and-aft, for a total of 56,000 square feet of canvas. The square sails were employed on the fore, main, and mizzen masts. The jigger carried fore-and-aft sails, as did the bowsprit. Several fore-and-aft sails were raised between the taller masts when full-suited.

Each vessel required a crew of about 30 men, including the captain, three mates, bos'n, carpenter, donkeyman, sail-maker, cook, messman, 10 or 12 ABs (ablebodied seamen), six ordinary seamen, and four young apprentices.

Both vessels had first class accommodations for captains and crews, according to J. Ferrell Colton in *Windjammers Significant*. In each case, the master, three mates, carpenter, donkeyman, sailmaker, cook, and steward occupied quarters in the amidship house, and the 24 foremast hands were in two forecastles, port and starboard, each with 12 bunks. The captain and chief mate had private rooms, and the others in the amidship house roomed two in a room.

Colton reported that "few steamers, including the *Queen Elizabeth* and *Queen Mary*, provided as fine quarters for their captains as did this class of nitrate barks. Both in space and appointments, their accommodations were most lavish. The areas allocated to the captain's use consisted of six rooms."

There was a small room for a pilot or guest. The captain had his own private bathroom and private stairway up to the bridge and chartroom directly overhead. Mahogany and exotic woods were used for woodwork and trim. Marble-topped brass-railed sideboards, mahogany tables seating up to 12 people, swivel chairs, settees, shelves holding potted plants, and skylights above were listed among the refinements.

The contract price of the ships was £435,885 (English pounds) the equivalent of $179,425 (U.S.) each, according to Colton. This was minuscule by today's standards, but impres-

German bark **Hans** *under tow from Glasgow shipyard to coal-loading berth in Wales, 1904. (From Colton collection.)*

sive in 1904. After they departed, William Hamilton & Co. built no more large windjammers.

Siemers & Co. assigned one of its favorite captains, Jurgen F. Kuelsen, to command the *Hans*, and he remained with his ship for 17 years, throughout the company's ownership. He made 10½ round trips between Europe and the West Coast during the first 10 years, and remained for seven years more during and after World War I.

On May 2, 1904, *Hans* was taken in tow for a coal port in Wales, where she loaded about 5,000 long tons of coal and coke for Iquique, Chile. A few days out, she was off the Canary Islands when an explosion and fire in the coal cargo forced her to turn back to Plymouth, England, to extinguish the flames, unload part of the cargo and make repairs.

She remained at Plymouth more than three months, finally sailing again September 9. She arrived at Iquique December 9, a passage of three months, considered reasonable for a heavily-loaded ship. After discharging, she shifted to Caleta Buena, January 5, 1905, and loaded 5,000 tons of nitrate for Hamburg.

During those first 10 years, *Hans* trekked forth and back between Hamburg, Wales, and the West Coast 10½ times, and made three extra round trips between the West Coast and Newcastle, Australia, for more coal. Two of the Australian voyages ended in Santa Rosalia, Baja California. She called at eight Chilean ports to deliver coal and coke, and load nitrate. Her owners tallied 72,000 long tons of coal and coke, and more than 50,000 tons of nitrate in her 24 cargoes. She was reported to have returned a fair profit.

Captain Kuelsen seldom pushed her like the smaller, lighter, heavily-canvased clippers which carried high-rated package cargoes at express speeds. She was designed and built for the Cape Horn nitrate run, but there were times, according to her log, that she caught up with and outran other vessels in the same trade.

On her last voyage west in 1914, *Hans* sailed March 4 from Hamburg, crossed the equator April 25, rounded Cape Horn June 9 (in midwinter), crossed the equator northbound in the Pacific July 1, and arrived of Cabo San Lucas, Baja California, July 21. She slowly beat up the Gulf of California against headwinds for five days, dropping anchor July 26 off Santa Rosalia. She had been underway 144 days, not a great record.

Herbert Tiesler, a young German AB on that final voyage, logged the trip in detail, as related by Captain Harold D. Huycke, Jr., in his fine book, *To Santa Rosalia, Further and Back*. Tiesler noted that June 9, when the ship rounded Cape Horn, Captain Kuelsen observed his birthday by inviting his crew to join him with bottled beer and "fancy sandwiches." Tiesler also said the ship had a good cook who produced tasty spiced gravies, good bread, lean salt pork, and fine pea soup.

The voyage turned out to be ill-fated for *Hans* and other German vessels which had come to Santa Rosalia with coal and coke briquets to fuel the smelter furnaces and railroad locomotives of the Compagnie du Boleo, the French-owned copper-mining concession.

Meanwhile, her sister, *Kurt*, which had arrived in Santa Rosalia June 12, slipped out of the harbor August 4 and successfully evaded Canadian men-o-war patrolling the Pacific sea lanes to arrive safely in the Columbia River September 11, anchoring off Astoria to await the time to load her chartered grain cargo.

Santa Rosalia proved to be a dismal place for the visiting German sailors. It was a town of about 10,000 Mexicans and Indians, who lived in wooden shacks scattered about the nearby arid hills. The sole industry was a big, dirty smelter, which melted down rich copper ore, called "boleo" in Spanish. The Mexican laborers and French supervisors had little regard for the Germans, who now were enemies of the French. The people were inhospitable at first.

Santa Rosalia is situated on the eastern side of the Baja Peninsula, about midway between the U.S. border and the tip at Cabo San Lucas. The whole area is a desert without shade or green growth, sparsely populated in 1914 by Indians. The town is about 430 miles south of San Diego and 340 miles north of LaPaz by modern highway, and with little between. The German sailors were trapped in an atmosphere they did not savor.

It was near Santa Rosalia in 1868 that a rancher picked up some nuggets that turned out to be copper carbonates and oxides. The ore proved to be rich, one of the richest deposits in the western world. Mining began in 1874 by German and Mexican miners, who shipped the ore outside for smelting. But a depression put a stop to their efforts. The French-owned Compagnie du Boleo took over the operations in 1885, shipping the first ore to Europe, but built a smelter the following year.

Railroads were built back to the mines in the hills, and ships brought in building materials and supplies from California and the Pacific Northwest. Homes were built for the workers and the town, but there were few of the amenities of city life.

After three ships were blown ashore by savage winds, the Boleo company started construction of breakwaters to enclose about one square mile of harbor for protection to the vessels bringing in the much-needed fuel for the furnaces. Work started in 1899 and was not completed until 1910. It cost the company $1 million—big money then.

Railroad tracks were laid on the breakwaters so cargo could be unloaded directly from ship to cars. However, Boleo company did not provide stevedores for unloading, so this work fell to the unlucky crew members of the ships, a chore unexpected and distasteful.

Boleo operated a sea-going steam bucket dredge in the harbor to dig out shoals and to act as a harbor tug to assist vessels in and out of the protected area. The company also operated a small steamship to make weekly runs 80 miles across the gulf to Guaymas on the eastern shore to pick up supplies and transport passengers.

This was the place where some 330 German sailors found themselves stranded at the outbreak of war. It was months later that the Germans felt secure in going ashore to mingle with unfriendly townspeople, and then the sailors went in groups for mutual protection. Some of the men knew former shipmates on the other ships and made occasional visits when off duty. Others paid-off or jumped ship to take the steamer to Guaymas to hitch-hike to more friendly parts of Mexico and the United States. Some stayed with their ships.

Captain Kuelsen and the other German masters tried to keep their vessels well-maintained and shipshape by keeping their men at work—at least those men who had not been paid-off or run away. Supplies, paint and funds ran low, and Captain Kuelsen made one trip to San Francisco to purchase supplies for the fleet.

The captains found time for daily get-togethers at the town's principal hotel, where they swapped stories over local beer, brooded about their personal problems and discussed world events, still expecting the Fatherland would become victorious.

As the war ran on, the days of sail ebbed. In the first place, many of the sailing vessels had been driven off the seas. Then, in August, 1914, the Panama Canal was completed to the extent that the first ship, the canal company's own S.S. *Ancon*, made the initial transit of the big ditch. When it opened for regular commercial traffic, the canal shortened distances between Europe and Chile by 5,000 nautical miles, and to western Mexico by 8,000 miles. It meant that steamships could make the trip in half the time, or less, than the poky sailers laboring around the Horn.

The Handsome *Hans* remained idle at Santa Rosalia until January 1921, and Captain Kuelsen was relieved of his command.

The *Hans* was not finished. She lived on to serve seven other owners, under three other names, sailed under two other flags, and made another memorable voyage around Cape Horn during another major world war.

Chapter 2

Waiting Out the War

When the *Hans* arrived in Santa Rosalia, she sailed into the midst of a bloody Mexican revolution that began in 1910 and continued for four years more as strong men battled for control. Victoriano Huerta, Venstiano Carranza and the bandit leader, Pancho Villa, were the principal contenders in 1914.

Villa and his army of irregulars and Yaqui Indians ranged throughout northern Mexico and occasionally made raids down the Baja peninsula as far as Santa Rosalia, overwhelming the Carranza federal garrisons, which in time regrouped and returned to drive out the Villa forces. The flag changed every few months.

When the barracks changed hands, the defenders fled to the hills or joined the opposition. Those who failed to depart in time or who refused to take up guns with the newcomers found themselves against a wall and shots ended their participation.

Thus it was that when the German sailors filed into town for beer and small talk at the Cantina de Leon or the Hotel Central Moderno, they occasionally met new faces in control. The Germans were not interested in local or national politics and prudently kept to themselves as much as possible. And the Mexican troops gave them little notice. The boys returned to their ships unmolested unless they got into brawls.

One of the quick changeovers occurred when an improvised gunboat slipped into the harbor between the idle German vessels and lobbed shells into the town, aimed at the barracks. The defenders departed for the hills as a band of 30 Yaquis disembarked and marched on the barracks.

One brawl became an international battle in the tavern of the Hotel Central Moderno, the fancier of the drinking places. A British steamer had arrived to load out copper matte and two American ships came, the coaster *Jim Butler* making her monthly supply visit, and a larger freighter with a cargo of coke and coal for the smelter. Their young men trooped up to the hotel, as sailors do, to sample the local beer and tequila, when some of the Germans, off duty, arrived.

A party started and somebody called for music. The local orchestra complied, according to Herbert Tiesler, the young AB from the *Hans*. The Mexican national anthem was sounded first, as was appropriate. Then came "Deutschland Uber Alles," and the Germans toasted their Fatherland, everybody standing. Next, the band played "God Save the King" for the Britishers. This was followed by the "Star Spangled Banner" for the Americans. All stood except the British.

Tiesler reported that a big American Scandinavian, who had already consumed his share of brew, ordered the British to "Stand oop." He was met with a curt "Go to 'ell."

As the Yankee reached out to help the nearest Limey to his feet, fists flew, and the war was on. Soon the Germans and Mexicans were in it, too, swinging chairs, tables, and bottles, and yelling their own native expletives. It took all the local police and some current militiamen to stop the battle. The jail was filled and the overflow fighters found themselves confined to caves, with barred doors, for the remainder of the night.

Stuck in this forlorn outstation, the young German naval reservists were unable to get paid-off or go farther than town limits, held back by strict German laws and rules. But some of the other nationals, particularly Danes, who were not bound by German rules, asked to be paid-off, even at half the regular pay due them. Captain Kuelsen of the *Hans* was considered senior among the captains and acted as consul to decide which men could depart.

During those early days of the war, the German light cruiser *Leipzig* slipped into the gulf and the port of Mazatlan in urgent need of coal. She was a vessel 341 feet long, with a crew of 286 and a top speed of 22 knots. She had bunker space for only 822 tons of coal and at top speed she consumed this amount in four days, hardly enough for a vessel playing hide and seek with the Australian cruiser *Newcastle* and the Japanese cruiser *Idzuma*, both larger and more heavily armed.

With the assistance of the German consul at Guaymas and a sympathetic businessman who saw the making of a profit, the *Leipzig* moved to the dock at Guaymas, filled her bunkers with coal and added more in sacks on deck, during a brief rendezvous. She disappeared over the horizon and escaped from the gulf before the Allied warships arrived. She went on down the west coast, picking up more coal from German vessels lying off Chilean ports, rounded Cape Horn and steamed into the South Atlantic, where a British naval fleet intercepted her and promptly sank her along with others under German Admiral Von Spee's command.

Men on the *Hans*, like those on the 10 other interned German ships in Santa Rosalia, were put to work maintaining their charges in preparation for an early culmination of the war and orders to load return cargoes. They were sent aloft to take down the sails to be dried, repaired and folded away for safety.

Then they were put to work cleaning, scraping and painting hulls. Some of the men built bulkheads lengthwise down the centers of holds and laboriously shoveled ballast from one side to the other to shift the weight and careen the vessels to raise one side several feet out of the water. This exposed barnacles and marine growth that had accumulated below the waterline. Barnacles and growth were scraped and pounded off and the cleaned surfaces painted, usually with two coats.

Then the ballast was shoveled back to raise the other side and the scraping and painting repeated. This was hard, tiresome work, but the German boys had some previous practice when they shoveled out 4,000 to 5,000 tons of coal and coke from each ship for the Compagnie du Boleo. With hulls in fair condition, the men attacked masts, spars, bowsprits, rigging, deckhouses and decks. After weeks of drudgery the men must have been proud and relished the brew consumed on shore.

The Boleo company continued to operate without the fine German coke preferred at the smelter. New supplies came from California, brought in by steam schooners under charter. Mexican copper was in demand by the warring nations, as well as the United States. The smelter was producing 3,000 tons of matte and ingots a month, and consuming twice that amount of fuel.

Some of the partially-refined copper was shipped across the Gulf to Guaymas for loading onto rail cars and delivered to New Orleans for further transport to Europe or eastern U.S. factories.

By the end of 1914, the big drive by the Kaiser's armies toward Paris had been blunted and it became apparent that the war would continue indefinitely. As the men on the ships learned this they became more restless and sought ways of leaving. The men had little money and could not go far. The trail over the hills was forbidding, but several men tried it as a way out, anyway.

Three men from one vessel started out together, but after a few days of near famine, no water, and unfriendly natives, two of them turned back to Santa Rosalia, and were incarcerated in the jail until bailed out by their unforgiving captain. The third man was swallowed up by the desert.

Another group of six young Danes found an old steam launch on the beach and put it back into running order. Deserting their ship one night they piled aboard with their few belongings and started out, apparently bound to the north end of the gulf and hopefully to the U.S.A. The pilot failed to see a mooring line stretched from a ship to a distant anchor and when the boat passed under it, the line swiped the tall stack of the small boat completely off. But the accident did not stop the launch and it continued out of the harbor and into the night.

A few weeks later, the boat was found beached about 30 miles north of town, but there was no sign of the men. Their fate was sealed in this barren, inhospitable land.

Some of the men were more resourceful and luckier. They awaited the opportunity to stow away on visiting neutral ships. The steam schooner *Jim Butler*, coming in from California, frequently was short-handed and her captain was not opposed to signing on new hands for the return trip to Los Angeles, San Francisco, or Portland. These men were not always paid, but at least they were delivered into a land of opportunity, where most of them found jobs, either afloat or ashore, and eventually became American citizens.

One Belgian ship picked up a couple of men in Santa Rosalia and kept them aboard until it arrived in Portland for a wheat cargo for England. The German crew members were left ashore in Portland and neutral seamen took their places.

Another way of getting out of town was offered by a friendly fat Dutchman, who became an agent between men and masters. He provided crews as needed and collected his reward from the captains of short-handed vessels. He met the Germans on the street or in taverns and told them about the wonders of the lands to be visited by the ships needing crews. He promised a better life. He bailed some men out of jail on their promises to sail on the next vessel leaving. He lived well, but some of the men found the ships were bound to much different climes than the Dutchman had promised.

Some of the men who paid-off at Santa Rosalia had enough pesos to make it to Guaymas on the cross-gulf ferry, but not enough to go farther. They wandered into the Yaqui valley, where enterprising German-American farmers had settled on land previously occupied by the Yaqui Indians. The Indians were resentful for being forced back into the hills and made raids on farms and farmers, killing and burning, then disappearing into the mountains.

The German boys found work on the farms and some of them saw promise in owning their own land. They had to arrange for supplies of water for irrigation from the regional water company. This led to disaster for one group of six young German and Austrian sailors, who set off one day to hike up the railroad track to the next village to interview the head of the water company.

On the way, a party of armed Yaquis appeared out of the brush and surrounded five of the men. The youngest of the group had fallen behind and hid in the brush until nightfall, when he returned to town without knowing the fate of his friends. The next day, searchers found the mutilated bodies of the five young men not far from where they were captured by the Yaquis.

A few days later, Yaquis stopped a train and massacred 250 passengers and the train crew.

The Gulf of California, now frequently known as the Sea of Cortez, is frequented by sudden severe storms borne on winds 75 to 100 miles per hour. One of these storms hit the Santa Rosalia area on January 1, 1915, about five months after the *Hans* arrived. It proved extremely damaging to the vessel when another Siemers ship, the 4-masted bark *Egon*, dragged her anchor.

Egon was swept downwind into the *Hans*, smashing into the latter's bowsprit, twisting it out of shape, upward from the forepeak, and bending it about 18 feet from the outer end. The bowsprit stabbed into *Egon*'s port quarter, went through the mate's room, smashed the poop and mangled deck gear. As *Egon* slid along the side of *Hans*, it flattened the *Hans*' steel bulwarks. Fortunately, nobody was hurt.

Egon finally came to rest abaft the *Hans* when its anchor grabbed. The storm abated as rapidly as it arrived. Crews of both vessels worked for several months repairing damage, and were assisted by men from other ships.

The damage to *Hans*' bowsprit proved to be more lasting than foreseen at the time. It resulted in this stately vessel being out of service for a total of 21 years, and long after coming under American ownership in 1920.

The United States entered the war on the side of the Allies April 6, 1917, and an American consular representative arrived soon afterward in Santa Rosalia to check on the German vessels interned there. He took steps to cut off ships and crews from supplies and food. However, the Germans had made friends among local people, who brought them food and necessities. Then came a rumor that the United States planned to seize the German vessels and tow them to sea and up the coast. The German embassy, still functioning in Mexico City, responded by advising the captains to prepare for dismantling critical equipment of their ships, or better, to sink them on the spot if any move was made to seize them.

The consul at Guaymas sent over a quantity of dynamite bombs and long fuses with instructions to plant the bombs at the feet of masts, to be exploded if necessary. The bombs were said to have remained in place until after the end of the war, November 11, 1918. No attempt was made by the U.S. to seize the vessels.

Meanwhile *Hans'* sister ship, *Kurt*, was seized at Astoria, Oregon, where she was interned early in the war, and given a new name, *Dreadnaught*, later changed to *Moshulu*, an Indian term, meaning "fearful" or "fearless." *Moshulu* was towed to Portland, put into seaworthy condition and assigned to Charles Nelson Co. of San Francisco for hauling lumber on the Pacific. Capt. Wilhelm Tonissen and the few Germans left on the ship were sent to a prison camp in Georgia for the remainder of the war.

When word of the war's end came to the Germans at Santa Rosalia, it was with difficulty that the captains and remaining crews could believe that the Fatherland had been defeated. As time passed they realized their homeland was prostrated. They hoped their ships soon would be moving again. But no charters came through, no orders for cargo. Funds for paying crews were almost non-existent, the ships were in poor condition and in dire need of drydocking.

In desperation, 70 of the men remaining signed a petition to Captain Kuelsen, representing the captains, asking for their status and for payment of wages due. Captain Kuelsen responded that they would be paid monthly in dollars, gold or pesos—whatever was available. This kept the men aboard although unhappy. Most were older men or naval reservists who remained loyal to their ships and masters.

Then came the word that the Allies were seizing all German shipping as reparations, with strict instructions for turn-over. Instead of coming for the vessels, the Allies decreed that the Germans were to sail the ships home to Germany or to Allied ports, for delivery.

German owners negotiated an agreement permitting them to load the vessels for the return voyages to help pay expenses. But crews had scattered and most of the ships were not in condition to sail. An abundance of war-built steam freighters filled the need for ocean cargoes, and freight rates began to slide. Sailing ships no longer were needed.

The crews at Santa Rosalia were heartened once by a San Francisco newspaper report that the laid-up fleet had been charted to load wheat at Portland, Oregon, for European destinations. Then the report turned out to be fictitious, and the victors in war began to divide up the loser's vessels. *Hans* was assigned to Great Britain.

Capt. Robert Dollar, head of the Dollar lumber empire, became interested in the former German sailing fleet and negotiated for the vessels. He acquired *Hans* for $27,000, the highest price offered for any of the fleet, and sent men and a towing vessel to Santa Rosalia to bring the *Hans* to San Francisco Bay. *Hans* was the queen of the fleet and first to be taken north. Captain Kuelsen and his remaining crew members returned to Germany via Guaymas and Vera Cruz.

When Captain Jurgen Friedrick Kuelsen arrived home to Hamburg he found the shipping industry devastated. He had been going to sea since he was 14. Now he was 53. He had served his four years in the Imperial Navy and became a merchant shipmaster at 28. He was 36 when he became captain of the *Hans*, and at 48 he was senior among the German captains at Santa Rosalia.

Back in Hamburg, Kuelsen already was aging from the long sojourn in Mexico. Jobs were scarce and he worked for a time as watchman over some laid-up sailing vessels. When G. J. H. Siemers & Co. reorganized and began to replace its lost fleet with several small freighters, Kuelsen went out as master in the North Sea and North Atlantic trades. He wound up his career as port captain for Siemers' post-war fleet and finally died of flu at the age of 59.

Chapter 3

Hans to *Mary Dollar* to *Tango*

When the big bark *Hans* was removed from the Santa Rosalia anchored fleet on the end of a towline, she ended 6½ years of enforced idleness. The war had dragged on for four years and three months, and post-war negotiations between nations over reparations lasted another two years and two months. Lumberman Robert Dollar dreamed of putting *Hans* and other big sailing ships to work hauling his lumber across the Pacific to Japan and China.

Dollar sent his port captain, Christian J. Fosen, to Santa Rosalia to prepare *Hans* and 10 other newly-purchased ships for towing to San Francisco Bay. Fosen liked the *Hans*, the newest in the idle fleet, and Dollar had paid more for her than any other—$27,000—so *Hans* was the first to be readied for the long tow to California. Captain Fosen picked up some German sailors still hanging around Mexico to help prepare the ship and to identify sails and other equipment bearing German names.

Hans had been allotted to Britain, so it was easy to transfer her registry to Dollar's Canadian representative, A. M. Dollar, at Vancouver, B.C., where the company had a large sawmill. However, the home port was not painted in, and British or Canadian flags were not raised, leaving it easy to later transfer registry to the United States. And *Hans* never visited Vancouver.

She had her twisted bowsprit, which Dollar determined would be costly to straighten or replace, so that task was put off while other recently-purchased former German barks were brought up from Santa Rosalia for close examination.

Hans soon had company as former fleetmates were laid alongside.

Hans, like the others, was given a coat of black paint, after a Dollar company practice. It covered up the identifying Siemers color scheme, which was accented by a broad white band along each side, broken by 18 square black patches resembling gunports on ancient men-of-war. The Siemers colors were streaked with rust from seven years of wear and neglect.

Soon after she was anchored, the *Hans* was given a close inspection by Captain P. A. McDonald, a well-respected West Coast sailing ship man in the employ of Dollar. McDonald liked the ship, but found some pitting in the shell plates which necessitated welding on a doubler plate or two. The bottom was heavily encrusted with marine growth. Otherwise, McDonald declared *Hans* in fine condition with the exception of the damaged bowsprit.

Dollar then gave the vessel a new name: *Mary Dollar*. It was Robert Dollar's practice to name his vessels after family members. Mary was a half-sister. The ship carried this name for 13 years, but no farther than a couple of tows across the bay and one down the coast to Wilmington, California. She was out of work all that time.

Although she was the most treasured member of the Dollar sail fleet, *Mary Dollar* remained at anchor while fleetmates were taken away. Four were cleaned, painted, repaired and conditioned for the China lumber trade, which petered out in about two years. Two of the ships eventually were left in China and cut down to barges for storage purposes on the Yangtze River.

As the post-war depression in shipping developed, the result of a vast over-supply of wartime-built steam freighters and sagging freight rates, Dollar sailing vessels became a drug on the market. Three or four were sold, rigged down and ended their days as barges hauling logs and lumber in British Columbia waters. Others were sold for scrap.

By 1929, the *Mary Dollar* was the only member of the Dollar sailing fleet. It had been moved several years before across the bay to an anchorage in Oakland Creek, near Alameda, and now was settled in a mud flat.

Robert Dollar continued to believe freight rates and general conditions would improve to allow his favorite big ship to go back to work. Then, in May 1932, he died at the age of 88. His company was busy operating a fleet of large passenger and freight steamships across the Pacific, around the world, and intercoastal. *Mary Dollar* was not needed and her value lessened every year.

The company considered the ship was too fine to scrap and sought ways of putting her to good use. It offered to donate her to the State of California for operation as a training ship for young seamen, even suggesting it might carry freight to help pay expenses. But California was suffering from depression blues and claimed it had no money for such extravagance. Later, however, it acquired a medium-sized steamship which it outfitted as a school ship. Dollar then offered the *Mary Dollar* to the State of Washington, but that state rejected the gift as too expensive.

With the market for aging sailing vessels steadily declining, Dollar finally sold the *Mary Dollar* to a semi-retired sailing ship master, Captain Charles A. Watts, of Berkeley, Cal., reputedly for $3,500. The transaction was closed October 3, 1934. Captain Watts did a little fixing-up on the vessel while it rested in the mud at Alameda, ostensibly in preparation for another stretch of sea duty. But then he had an opportunity to resell the vessel to southern California gambling interests, incorporated in Carson City, Nevada, as SS *Tango* (Nev.).

Captain Watts moved the ship back across the bay to Sausalito and prepared her for a tow to Wilmington. He hired the steam schooner *Dan F. Hanlon* to make the tow, and hired a crew of six deckhands, a mate and a cook.

The *Hanlon* towed the *Mary Dollar* out of the bay in the face of a strong southeast gale, despite warnings that the going would be rough. The big empty sailing vessel pitched, tossed, and rolled savagely in the heavy seas outside the Golden Gate as if in an effort to cast off her towline. And that is just what she did off Point Montara, about 12 miles south of the gate. The towline snapped. The steamer was pitching and rolling unmercifully and was unable to get back to the *Mary Dollar*. In fact, it was all she could do to get back through the Golden Gate and safety from the storm.

The *Mary Dollar* was left at the mercy of the seas, but her new captain and owner was quick to take preventive measures before the ship could be blown ashore on a cruel and rocky coast or farther to sea. He and his crew pulled some old sails out of the 'tween decks and jury-rigged them sufficiently to make good use of the wind. They sailed northward 40 miles to Drake's Bay, dropped anchors and radioed for help.

A staunch ocean tug, the *Sea Monarch*, came out from San Francisco when the wind quieted and put her towline on the distressed sailing ship. They turned south and arrived in Wilmington three days later, berthing at the Patton-Blinn Lumber Company wharf.

The new owners gave a new name, *Tango*, to the vessel. she was rigged down. Her tall steel masts were cut away and stacked with her 18 steel yards, the bent bowsprit, the fine amidship deckhouse and bridge, and her steel bulwarks on the wharf to be picked up by the nearby Alaska Salvage Company and scrapped. That ended her career as a handsome four-masted bark. She was destined to become a glittering gambling barge, but unsightly in spite of her bright lights, anchored at sea in Santa Monica Bay—sort of a painted floozy.

To rebuild the newly-named *Tango* into a gambling barge, the new owners had the main deck cleared from forecastle to poop and built on it a large barnlike structure some 280 feet long by 50 feet or more wide, extending a few feet over each

Gambling barge **Tango** *anchored off Long Beach, California, 1935-39. This shows the ocean side. The landing platform was on the lee side facing the land. Tony Cornero, one of the original operators, differed with his partners on how to operate. He offered to buy them out and they refused. He then suggested one roll of dice for all or nothing. He lost. (From Ernest Marquez collection.)*

Interior of the gambling barge **Tango**, *following a raid July 27, 1935. Another gambling room for "high rollers" was made in the holds by shoveling ballast sand behind partitions to make space for a large room. It had plush carpets and was available only to rich gamblers who wanted to gamble in private. (From Ernest Marquez collection.)*

side. This building housed the gambling machinery, gaming tables, lounges, rest rooms and other accommodations for patrons. To stabilize the ship at sea, 500 tons of sand was poured over the copper slag loaded aboard during *Hans*'s Santa Rosalia days. Then the hull was painted gray, a large "Tango" sign was painted on each side and outlined with sparkling lights.

Tango was not the first gambling ship to anchor out just beyond the three-mile limit off the Greater Los Angeles west shore. Other vessels were already there, as well as some deepsea fishing barges. One was the *Johanna Smith*, a small wooden steam schooner. Another was a cement-built ship renamed *Monte Carlo*. A third was the *Rex*, the former 300-foot four-masted bark *Star of Scotland*, ex-*Kenilworth*, built in Glasgow in 1887. Water taxis hustled patrons out from Long Beach and Wilmington to the gambling ships.

The gambling ship operators were bitter rivals and mysterious fires and deep-sea holdups and robberies occurred. The *Johanna Smith* was destroyed by fire. The *Monte Carlo* slipped her anchor cable and drifted ashore. The *Casino*, a former barkentine, drifted ashore and burned.

The owner of the *Johanna Smith* sought a larger vessel and found the *Mary Dollar*, which he purchased from Captain Watts. By 1939, the *Tango* and the *Rex* were the principal gambling ships off Santa Monica Bay. They were lighted up at night to be seen from the coastal towns of Redondo Beach and Santa Monica. By that time a small steamer of various names, lately the *Star of Hollywood*, now the *Texas*, was in the vicinity.

The owner of the *Rex*, a somewhat notorious figure, Tony Cornero, advertised widely and hired sky-writers to draw patrons to his ship. He stationed men at horse racing tracks to relay the race results by radio to the ship and promote his betting activities. Federal authorities were not greatly concerned with what went on at sea, but state officials noted that Cornero was cutting into the state's profits from pari-mutuel betting at the race tracks. The state was drawing a nice percentage from the horse betting, but nothing from the anchored ships.

That was when Earl Warren, then California's attorney-general, went to court in an effort to put the ships out of business. He succeeded in having the three-mile limit moved out to a line from Point Vincente to Point Dume, west of Santa Monica, which placed the gambling ships inside the line. It forced the ships to move out into water too deep for anchoring and farther from their shoreside bases.

Cornero resisted and continued to operate until state police, sheriff's officers, and coastguard men came out and boarded the *Rex*, putting it out of business. *Tango* and *Texas* gave up peacefully. *Texas* remained outside as a legal fishing barge, but *Tango* and *Rex* were towed in to San Pedro and retired as sea-going gamblers.

That began two more years of idleness for the *Tango*, ex-*Mary Dollar*, ex-*Hans*, making up a total of 20 years of collecting barnacles.

As World War II heated up and the demand for cargo space increased, the value of anything that would float went up and up. A strong market for Pacific Coast lumber developed in South Africa after the normal supply from Finland and northern Europe was cut off by U-boat activities. Ocean freights sky-rocketed.

Shipping men and investors envisioned an opportunity for profits if they could find hulls to haul lumber to South Africa. They found about six old hulls along the West Coast, some of them reduced to barges, but redeemable as sailing vessels. Sailers under neutral flags were ideal for the South African lumber trade.

The aging *Star of Finland*, a 225-foot steel vessel built in 1889 at Bath, Maine, was purchased from the Alaska Packers by D. H. Bates, a Portland insurance man, who soon resold it to San Francisco operators. She was renamed *Kaiulani* (its original name), registered in Panama, and loaded in Grays

Harbor with lumber for Durban. She sailed on to Hobart and Sydney, Australia, where the U.S. Army acquired her and downrigged her into a barge for supplying troops in the Southwest Pacific.

The schooner *Vigilant*, a World War I wooden product, 241 feet long and 1603 gross tons, was renamed *City of Alberni* in 1941 and sailed with 1,800,000 board feet of lumber for South Africa. She suffered a beating off Cape Horn and returned to Valparaiso, Chile, in leaking condition. After the war, she was renamed *Condor* and sailed around the Horn to Montevideo with a cargo of rice.

The schooner *Commodore*, another wartime wooden hull, 232 feet long, 1526 gross tons, loaded lumber at Port Angeles, Washington, and made a successful voyage to Cape Town and Durban early in 1942, but ran into hard times and was sold to cover debts.

Another wartime Cape Horner was the *Daylight*, which had been hulked into a barge in the 1920s and was rerigged by Canadian owners as a "stump-masted staysail auxiliary barkentine." She made it safely to South Africa with a cargo of Canadian lumber and explosives.

Then came the *Star of Scotland*, given back her old Alaska Packers name after the gambling days under the name of *Rex*. She was rerigged in California as a six-masted schooner and loaded her lumber cargo in Grays Harbor. She sailed in February 1942, with a crew of 17, and made it safely to Cape Town. She remained there until November when she sailed for Brazil with a cargo of coal.

When out a few days from Cape Town, she was accosted by a German submarine which had surfaced and ordered the crew into lifeboats. The U-boat then shelled the schooner and sank her on an unlucky Friday, the 13th of November. The only casualty was the mate, who fell in and drowned while launching a lifeboat.

An interesting aftermath was an example of "comradeship of the sea" reported in W. H. McCurdy's *Marine History of the Pacific Northwest, 1896-1965,* edited by Gordon Newell. When Germany was broken and starving after the war, Captain Constantine Flink, of the *Star of Scotland,* remembered Captain Witte, commander of the U-boat, and sent him several packages of food and clothing, according to Newell.

New York and Boston investors became interested in the South African lumber trade and envisioned the makings of fancy profits. They incorporated the Transatlantic Navigation Co. during the summer of 1941 and sent Captain Asa F. Davison, former mate of the bark *Kenilworth,* later the *Star of Scotland,* to scout the West Coast in search of one or more suitable vessels. Captain Davison found the *Tango* laid up in Wilmington and after a quick inspection bought her for his company, reportedly for $25,000. TNC became the fifth owner in 37 years.

The *Tango* was moved to the Outer Harbor Dock & Wharf Co. to be refitted for sea duty. First, the ballast had to be discharged to permit an inspection of the inner hull. Representatives of the new owners estimated there was 500 tons of Mexican copper slag and about 650 tons of sand in the bottom, but it turned out to be more like 2,500 tons. The big gambling house was torn off and the vessel stripped to its main deck. One of the principal owners, Mr. Ossit Pernikoff, came from New York to stand by during the rejuvenation and loading of the vessel.

J. Ferrell Colton was one of the experts hired to plan and reconstruct the vessel. He had acquired a knowledge of the *Tango*'s hull configuration when he served as a member of the crew of the *Moshulu,* the former *Kurt,* sister of the *Hans/Tango,* a few years before. He was employed as an advisor on hull, rig, and sail plans, and other details. He was instrumental in locating drydocking plans for the *Moshulu* at Victoria, B.C., and these were indispensable in drydocking the *Tango* later. The ship had not been drydocked since its last visit to Hamburg in 1914 and no U.S. yards had plans for this hull.

Fir mast for **Tango** *being turned at Portland Spar Co., August, 1941. (Barber)*

Colton stated in his book that he hoped and suggested that the *Tango* be rigged as a four-masted barkentine, using the same deck holes for masts as the vessel had when she was a bark. He proposed that a 65-foot bridge and crew quarters be built amidships as in the *Hans/Mary Dollar* days, and other work be performed to return the ship to its pre-*Tango* condition.

But Colton's suggestions were over-ruled by higher authority. The owners wanted a simple sail plan to keep the crew down to a minimum and save expenses. Instead, the vessel was rerigged as a six-masted bald-headed schooner, a simple design that would not require a large crew of agile young men to climb high to the yards for handling square sails. The plan proposed a crew of 17 compared to 30 for a square-rigger.

The suggestion for a big amidship deckhouse was rejected and quarters were provided in the forecastle for the deck crew, in the poop for the captain and mates, and in a new small deckhouse aft the fifth mast for the cook, messman, radio operator, carpenter and galley. A small addition was built to the forecastle to provide necessary crew quarters.

The main deck was left open between the mainmast and spanker mast to permit a sizable deckload, which meant more revenue for the owners.

Some consideration was given to renaming the vessel *Marie*, but the idea was dropped to save money and red tape.

Tango was lifted on a floating drydock at the Los Angeles Shipbuilding and Drydock Corp., September 4, 1941. During the ensuing week some 40 tons of barnacles and marine growth were scraped off the hull. The bottom was sandblasted and drilled with 161 small holes to check on the condition and thickness of plates. The hull was found to be in excellent condition despite numerous pits under the turns of the bilges. Many of these were spot-welded and 19 doubling plates were welded over thin steel. Leaky rivets were welded over. A coat of paint prepared the vessel for undocking and she went back into the water September 10.

At the San Pedro Lumber Co. dock, new hatches were cut through the deck, new mast holes were cut, new coamings and bulwarks were built, new deck houses built and new quarters installed in the poop.

The United States entry into the war December 7, 1941, did not slow the work, but added incentive to hurry it. Moved back to the Outer Harbor dock, the ship received six steel butts for its masts. These tubes, 63 feet long and 30 inches in diameter, had been salvaged from a Wyoming oil drilling operation. They were set on the keelson and towered more than 30 feet above the deck.

Into these tubes were inserted the butt ends of Douglas fir masts 108 feet long and straight as an arrow. The timbers had been cut from trees felled near Westport, Oregon, and were turned by the Portland Spar Co., in Portland. The same plant provided the masts for the *Star of Scotland* and other rerigged ships. The *Star*'s masts were built in two sections, one being 100 feet long, the other 60 feet long, with 10 feet provided for scarphing. Five red hot steel bands were shrunk on the scarphs to provide for 150-foot masts.

Tango's masts were single timbers set in the steel butts to provide a total height of 165 feet above the keelson. Masts for the vessels were transported to Los Angeles on three flat cars, two to carry the ends and the middle car to hold the train together. Booms and gaffs also came from the fir forests of Oregon and were turned by Portland Spar Co.

Each mast of the *Tango* was supported by six wire shrouds on each side. A new 70-foot fir bowsprit was installed at St. Helens.

While *Tango* was being resurrected, her new captain arrived. He was Captain Carl B. Gundersen, of Brooklyn, N.Y., a Norwegian native and a veteran in sail. His last command was James A. Farrell's 261-foot full-rigged iron-

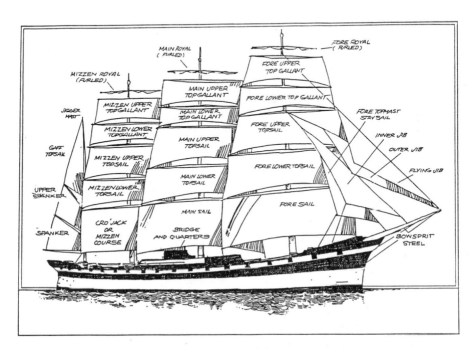

Sail Plan of S.V. *Hans/Mary Dollar,* **1904-1934**

These are the principal working sails of a four-masted bark. When in full canvas, the royals were raised to the masthead; here are furled, as was common. Two or three fore-and-aft staysails were hung between the fore and main masts, the main and mizzen masts, and the mizzen and spanker masts. The full suit comprised 35 sails covering 56,000 square feet.

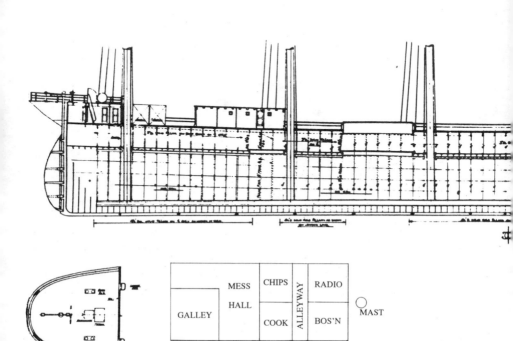

		MESS	CHIPS		RADIO	
GALLEY		HALL	COOK	ALLEYWAY	BOS'N	MAST

DECKHOUSE AFT

POOP DECK

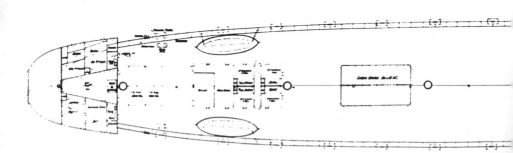

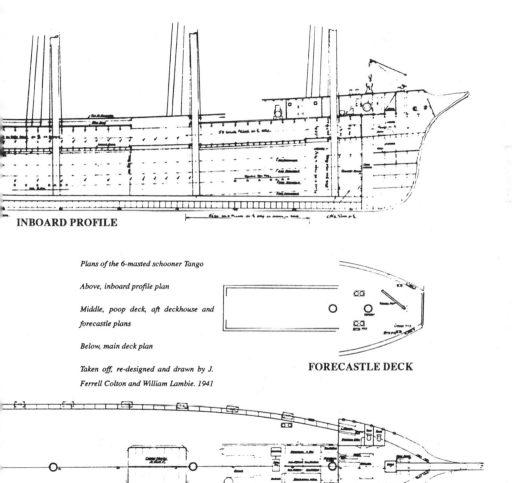

INBOARD PROFILE

Plans of the 6-masted schooner Tango

Above, inboard profile plan

Middle, poop deck, aft deckhouse and forecastle plans

Below, main deck plan

Taken off, re-designed and drawn by J. Ferrell Colton and William Lambie. 1941

FORECASTLE DECK

MAIN DECK PLAN

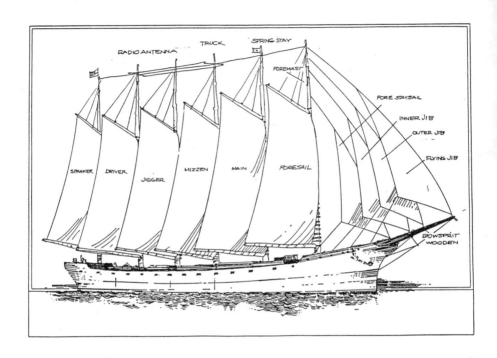

Sail Plan of the S.V. *Tango/Cidade do Porto,* 1942-1946

When restored as a six-masted bald-headed schooner, the **Tango** *had a simple set of six large sails, 102 feet by 46 feet in size, which were interchangeable, and four jib sails as shown here. She had no top sails. Total sail area was 33,000 square feet. This simple rig saved much manpower and expense for the owners, but was difficult for the limited crew to handle.*

hulled ship *Tusitala*. The vessel originally was the British ship *Inveruglas*, built in 1883 at Greenock, England.

The name "Tusitala" was a Polynesian term for "Teller of Tales," applied to Robert Louis Stevenson, who lived several years in Apia, Western Samoa. The ship eventually passed into the hands of the United States Maritime Commission and was laid up from 1938 until 1948 when it was scrapped.

Early in 1942, when the United States had been at war against Japan and Germany for more than a month, the *Tango* was towed up the Pacific Coast to the Columbia River, where it was berthed at the Pope & Talbot Company's lumber dock, in St. Helens, Oregon, 30 miles downriver from Portland. It lay there for about two months while rigging was completed and the big sails were delivered by truck from Long Beach, where they had been made to order. They were 102 feet long and 46 feet wide, and gaff-rigged. Three extra sails were provided. When fully-rigged, the vessel carried 33,000 square feet of canvas.

The set consisted of the flying jib, outer jib, inner jib, forestaysail, all raised from the bowsprit; fore, main, mizzen, jigger, driver and spanker sails.

During April, under charter to J. J. Moore & Co., 3,110,000 board feet of Douglas fir lumber was stuffed into the holds and lashed down on deck of the *Tango*.

This was the bulkiest cargo the vessel ever carried. The vessel was the largest six-masted schooner in the world, and the largest sailing vessel in the American Merchant Marine.

Chapter 4

St. Helens and Astoria

At St. Helens, the *Tango* berthed for more than a month at the Pope & Talbot company's long wharf while riggers and mechanics from Albina Engine & Machine Works, Portland, completed rigging the six towering masts stepped at San Pedro and installed the new Douglas fir bowsprit. The 69-foot timber had come from the Pope & Talbot forest lands in the Oregon coastal range near Westport, a mill town on the Columbia River 35 miles downstream from St. Helens. It was more than two feet in diameter at the butt, which was anchored in the forecastle head, and extended 56 feet from the bow. It was tapered toward the forward end and angled upward at 20 degrees.

Rigging included installation of stays and shrouds to support the masts. A steam donkey engine which had served time in the woods was installed on the forward deck to power the windlasses used in loading and unloading and to assist in raising sails. Some minor finishing was necessary in the Spartan crew quarters and the galley-messroom house aft.

Loading of the ship began early in April and was expedited by a gang of local longshoremen. One of these men was Fred Bitte, 31, of St. Helens, who had been working along the waterfront for a dozen years and joined the *Tango* crew as carpenter, donkeyman, and general mechanic. He had worked on Wilbur Smith's tugboats, in his uncle's Floating Marine Ways drydock and marine shop in Portland, and in the woods, as well as longshoring, gaining a wealth of knowledge and experience that became useful on the big sailing vessel during her long voyage.

Tango *at St. Helens loading dock. Rigger high on foremast. (Barber)*

The lumber cargo was stacked on the wharf beside the ship, conveniently located for moving in bundles to the nearby deck. Longshoremen stowed it piece by piece in the holds, working through hatches none too large. When the holds were stuffed full, added timbers were stacked on the open deck between the main and spanker masts to a height of about six feet. They were lashed down with chains and cables to prevent them from shifting and sliding in heavy weather.

This was heavy lumber, mostly two inches thick, a foot wide and in varying lengths, to be used for shoring up tunnel walls and ceilings in coal and diamond mines in the Drakensberg Mountains behind Durban, South Africa. They were heavy pieces and required two men to handle them. Loading was slow and carried on under the watchful eyes of Ossit Pernikoff, one of the owners, and his representative, Capt. Asa F. Davison.

The deck crew was hired from the Sailors Union of the Pacific in Portland during the last two weeks of loading. The vessel's owners and agents signed an agreement to use a full union crew, and the men had to be paid-up union members before they could sign-on. The captain and mates were non-union and this caused some problems because Captain Gundersen had worked previously with non-union crews and expressed disdain of this union crew and the rules it followed.

The Chief Mate was Peter L. Holt, of Brooklyn, N.Y., who held a master's papers and had commanded sailing ships. He was a short, squat man with a bully mate's expression, and the crew quickly dubbed him "Wolf Larsen."

Wages paid the ABs (ablebodied seamen), were reported to be $310 a month; ordinary seamen $257.50; boatswain, $245; radio operator and cook, $425. Captains of this class of vessel received $1,000 a month and chief mates $500 to $700. The *Tango* scale was higher than other sailing vessels that had departed in the same service previously. Total cost of the crew was believed to have been in the neighborhood of $6,000 a month.

One of the men inherited by Captain Gundersen was the youthful Ira Cheney, a Connecticut college boy so engrossed with sailing vessels that he stowed away on the *Tango* when it left San Pedro for the Columbia River. He was a member of a prominent Down East sailing family. His father was reputed to be a shipmaster and a distinguished ancestor was Donald McKay (1810-1880), who built 90 clipper ships, including the fastest of all, the *Flying Cloud*, which sailed around Cape Horn from New York to San Francisco in 89 days.

With this background, young Cheney insisted upon going to sea under sail despite his family's efforts to provide him a college education and turn him in another direction. He would skip classes and go down to the nearest harbor to ogle new vessels in port, and even traveled to Maine to look over a rotting hulk he heard was for sale. His family shipped him off to California with a new car and new clothes to get him away from New England's ships.

But, when Ira learned about the *Tango* being rigged for a long ocean voyage he dropped his studies, sold the car and clothes, went to San Pedro and disappeared aboard the ship. Two days later when the vessel was well out at sea and he was hungry, he appeared on deck ready to work his way. He was in his glory.

Stowaways are not usually welcome, but this young man of determination and good disposition made a place for himself. Captain Gundersen liked him although he had no previous sailing ship experience. When the crew was being selected for the *Tango*, Ira begged for a place and the good captain arranged a berth for him as ordinary seaman. Cheney had to join the union to become a crew member.

Later during the voyage, some of the more dedicated union members became suspicious of Cheney and black-balled him from their union meetings on the grounds that he was carrying tales to the captain. He was allowed back in meetings later when he agreed to abide strictly by union rules

Loading scene at St. Helens. Steam donkey engine at right provided power for lifting lumber bundles aboard. (Barber)

Rigger working high on foremast of **Tango**, *April, 1942. (Barber)*

and not tattle to the captain. He remained with the ship for more than two years and was one of the last men to leave when it was sold in Africa.

But the sea finally took this young man's life. He was lost while attempting to sail a 100-foot schooner single-handed down the Atlantic Coast to Florida. He disappeared in a storm. Only wreckage was found.

Another crew member was Archibald D. McPhee, of Portland, who learned by grapevine that the *Tango* was loading at St. Helens and signing a crew.

"I was working in the Willamette Iron & Steel Company's shipyard as a rigger and drawing good pay," he recalled. "We earned overtime pay by hiding out under the ways, but this got to be boring. As a boy I had read stories about life at sea and in sail, and I became enamored of it. I decided to get a berth on the *Tango* if possible. I had gone to sea previously on States Steamship Co. freighters, the *Michigan, W. R. Keever* and *North King*, and I carried AB papers.

"I had a 30-day shipping card from the union. When it was nearly expired I was in line for the next job on board. The *Tango* came up on the 29th day and I signed. My boss at the shipyard said I could not quit, but I did anyway. I went out on the *Tango* for the romance of going to sea in one of the last big sailing vessels.

"Before we sailed I was on the wharf at St. Helens with my bride, Ferne—we had been married only a few weeks before I sailed—and a dock watchman told my wife I was crazy to go on that ship. But we made it—a great experience. I'd do it again."

Of the crew, only five men had previous sailing ship experience. They were Hans Moller, Angelo Varellas, Charles Carlson, Chuck Hammer, and Jimmy Burke, all of them ABs. Most of the others were former steamship hands. They were George St. Clair, Howard Jones, Joe Kaplan and Archie McPhee, all ABs; and Mural Lee Rowley, O.S. (ordinary seaman). Ira Cheney and Fred Bitte had not been at sea.

Captain Carl B. Gundersen with family portrait on day **Tango** *sailed from St. Helens, April 29, 1942. (Barber)*

The cook, Charles LeMon, had been paroled from a prison term on his promise to go to sea, according to other crew members. The young radio operator, Gene Luce, 18, was a native of Scotts Bluff, Nebraska, who had been attending a radio school in Seattle, when the ship job came up. He was not a sailor, but soon became one. The other crew member, Bill Hahn, messboy, reportedly had not been at sea before.

All this loading, rigging, and sailing of the *Tango* was done without publicity or fanfare. America was at war and news about ships and their movements was closely censored.

This writer, then "covering the waterfront" as Marine Editor of the Portland *Oregonian*, heard about the presence of the big sailing ship at St. Helens through waterfront gossip.

Original crew of Tango, left to right, Front row: Temporary cook, messman, Angelo Varellas, Charles Hammer, Peter Holt, Capt. Carl D. Gundersen, Jimmy Burke, Back row: Howard Jones, Mural L. Rowley, Ira Cheney, Joe Kaplan, George St. Clair, Hans Moller, Fred Bitte, Archie McPhee, Charles Carlson, Radio operator Gene Luce and permanent cook joined at Astoria. (Barber)

I took time off from covering the busy Portland shipyards to drive to St. Helens to see what was going on there. I found that nobody who did not have business on board the vessel was allowed aboard.

On sailing day, April 29, however, after all cargo was lashed down, crew on board and two tugs standing by, Captain Gundersen invited me aboard to take some last minute pictures and get brief interviews. A smattering of relatives, townspeople, shippers and officials had gathered on the dock.

Captain Gundersen and I lined up the crew for a group photo and I got a few pot shots elsewhere on board—such as Ira Cheney and Swede Rowley, the ordinaries, at the door to their tiny room in the forepeak, and the captain at his desk in the poop. Then, back on the dock, I photographed the departure as the *Tango* was towed out into the river, turned around and headed downriver toward Astoria, the *Arrow No. 3* on the towline and the *Knappton* lashed alongside.

When the ship left St. Helens, she was shy three regular crew members. The radio operator was on his way from New York and a temporary cook and messman went only as far as Astoria, where they were replaced.

Came the final sailing day from Astoria to sea, May 3, 1942, exactly 38 years and one day after this same ship, then the four-masted bark *Hans*, sailed from her birthplace, the Glasgow, Scotland, shipyard.

I was present and was invited aboard the Columbia River Bar Pilots' schooner *Peacock* to accompany the *Tango* to sea. The same two tugs took the ship in tow, the pair in tandem out front as the entourage passed slowly by the town and into the channel to the river entrance. Leading the way was a Navy minesweeper because the river mouth was mined, leaving an unmarked channel for ship passage.

On the way down the channel, about 11 miles to the bar, a local amateur movie photographer, a friend of the pilots, and I were put into a small boat and rowed over to the *Tango*. Allowed aboard, we photographed members of the crew

Modest galley in **Tango**. *Cook prepares first meal. (Barber)*

Tug **Knappton** *leading and* **Arrow No. 3** *on tow line towing* **Tango** *to sea, bound for South Africa. (Barber)*

Tango *raising sails as seen from pilot boat* **Peacock**. *(Barber)*

View down deck of Tango, bound to sea. Ordinary Seaman Ira Cheney III and local cameraman in foreground. (Barber)

preparing to raise sails, the Captain, Pilot Elton Gillette, Mate Peter Holt, and two helmsmen at the big steering wheel on the poop; and the tugs and minesweeper out ahead. Then we were taken back to the pilot boat.

This sailing day was mild and clear, except for a few scattered clouds off to the northwest. The tug *Knappton* was not certified for ocean duty and dropped her towline at the bar, returning to port, but the *Arrow No. 3* kept a strain on her line until she had the vessel out near the lightship, about six miles from the bar. A light breeze played with the sails as they were raised one by one.

Upon a signal from the *Tango*, the *Arrow No. 3* slacked her line and her pilot, Capt. Clarence Ash, was picked up by the pilot schooner's small boat. Captain Gillette was taken from the *Tango*, and we started back to Astoria. *Tango* was on her own, with four huge sails and four smaller sails raised. Two of the large sails were raised later, after the steam donkey was fired up again. This was the only time all 10 sails were up, according to Fred Bitte.

We watched *Tango* fade away into the sunset.

I returned to Portland, typed a story which we hoped would pass censorship, and made up a set of pictures. These were turned over to a local censor, who mailed them to Washington for perusal by higher authority. Several weeks later they came back, well blue-penciled. Cut out were all the dates, the destination and route. Left in were the name of the vessel, a bit about the cargo, and some history of the ship.

The rest of the story about the voyage of this largest six-masted schooner in the world came back piecemeal from crew members who returned home in later years. Most of it came after the war had ended, the vessel had been sold in East Africa and had been given a new name.

Chief Mate Peter Holt and Captain Carl B. Gundersen get "shot" last time before leaving Columbia River. (Barber)

Tango and Arrow No. 3 part company off Columbia River. Crew had only four main sails raised because donkey engine ran out of steam. Foresail and spanker were raised later. (Barber)

Heading into the sunset off Columbia River. (Barber)

Chapter 5

Tango Around the Horn

From the Columbia River, the *Tango* followed a course recommended by the U.S. Navy as the safest way to avoid enemy warships or submarines, which had been reported off the west coast. The ship sailed southwesterly from the lightship and moved out well beyond the normal coastal shipping lane. She passed at least 100 miles west of San Francisco and widened her angle from the coast as she moved southward.

Off the Mexican coast she was two or three hundred miles from shore and she passed west of the Galapagos Islands, more than 1,500 miles offshore June 5, 33 days after leaving Astoria. Continuing southerly, *Tango* passed through the "Gay Twenties," the "Dirty Thirties," the "Roaring Forties," and the "Howling Fifties" as it sailed toward the tip of South America.

When Captain Gundersen ordered the helmsman to swing the vessel southeast toward Cape Horn, *Tango* was still 1,500 miles from the Horn and 1,000 miles or more west of southern Chile. The weather had become more severe and bitter cold. Antarctic storms and mountainous seas battered the vessel, ripped the sails, shifted the lumber deck cargo and thoroughly chilled the busy crew, which worked night and day to keep control. There was much handling of sails, raising, lowering, mending as necessary. Sometimes the men worked around the clock.

On June 26 the captain asked the lookouts to keep a sharp eye for icebergs. The men watched closely but reported only floating ice chunks in Antarctic waters.

Finally, July 10, 68 days from Astoria, Captain Gundersen announced that the ship had passed Cape Horn at a safe distance and could turn northeasterly toward warmer and less boisterous climes. The vessel then was close to the 60th parallel, the worst place in the world to be in the midst of an Antarctic winter. Not another vessel or bit of land had been sighted since leaving the Columbia River lightship.

Tango surged on northeasterly, passing east of the Falkland Islands and later between Gough and Nightingale Islands in the Tristan de Cunha group, more than 1,200 miles west of the Cape of Good Hope.

The ship arrived at Cape Town August 16, 105 days out of Astoria, a very respectable run for a heavily loaded big old schooner with an undermanned pick-up crew. By comparison, the *Star of Scotland*, also a six-masted schooner, but smaller and carrying less cargo, required 127 days to sail from Grays Harbor, Washington, to Cape Town, virtually the same distance covered by *Tango*. The *Star* was two months ahead of Tango and missed the worst weather.

Captain Gundersen and First Mate Peter Holt took the sights and kept the official ship's log, so the rest of the crew did not know exactly where they were unless they asked.

I made an effort to find the official ship's log, but without success. The Coast Guard Office of Merchant Marine Records in Washington, D.C., reported it did not have the log. I wrote to the Transatlantic Navigation Co., at 28 West 44th Street, New York City, hoping somebody would reply, but the letter was returned by the New York Post Office, marked "addressee unknown." Out of business.

I checked with Captain Gundersen's daughter, Mrs. Randi R. Norsell, Murphy, N.C., and her brother, Capt. Christian J. Gundersen, Tallahassee, Fla., but neither had a copy.

National Archives, Washington, D.C., reported that many logs of World War II vessels were stored in the Federal Records Center in New York City until 1974, when they were shredded under provisions of the Federal Records Act of

1970. That may have been the fate of *Tango*'s official log. Or it may have gone into a wastebasket.

So now we rely on the detailed day-by-day "log" kept by Archie McPhee and the diary kept by crewman Fred Bitte for the story of *Tango*'s last long voyage under sail. They kept a fine record of what went on on *Tango*'s deck, but give only infrequent mention of the vessel's actual position as kept by the captain.

McPhee detailed the crew's hard work, the fun, the fights, the bum food, and fears of the men. He was a big, strong, husky young man and was not challenged for fights as were others, but he declared later he broke up some fisticuffs.

Bitte was evidently homesick for his family—wife, Margaret, and small sons, Steve and Larry—about whom he wrote frequently while at sea. He played rummy with "Sparks," young Gene Luce, and lost, buying milkshakes for the winner after the ship arrived in Cape Town.

Sailors are more or less individualists and when they are closeted close together, as were the ten deck men on the *Tango*, disagreements and hard feelings arise. Within a week after leaving the Columbia River, minor matters became major ones. There was much bickering and hard feelings between the two watches, the Starboard Watch and Port Watch. They complained about the food and decided the cook was not a cook after all, but instead a pantryman and pastry cook. The cook refused to provide lunches for the night watch and tried to forbid the men to use the galley at night. The mess boy was seasick much of the time and became insubordinate, according to McPhee. The Captain squelched him.

By the time *Tango* arrived at the Equator, June 5, there was so much bitterness on the ship that no attempt was made to hold a Neptune's Court to initiate men who had never before crossed the line, as is customary on many vessels, large and small.

In that Equatorial region, some of the men got great pleasure out of standing naked under the water that cascaded down from the sails during tropical rainpours. They took baths and washed their clothes in the rain, and they caught water for the fresh water tank, ending rationing. "It was great," reported McPhee.

Ten days beyond the Equator, a severe storm threatened to blow out some sails. The mizzen got out of control and several men dropped the lines they had been holding. But not Ira Cheney. The college boy hung on desperately and was whipped up off the deck and out over the ocean. When he came back another blast shook him off and he fell 15 feet to the deck, spraining both arms and bloodying his nose. He was in the ship's hospital for three weeks. None of the men aboard had first aid training, but they attempted to doctor the young man to the best of their knowledge. McPhee bound him with tape, "butterfly fashion." He said he had read about how to do it. Apparently the effort worked out satisfactorily because Cheney was back on deck in about three weeks and became a lookout.

In good weather McPhee and others in the crew caught albatrosses, which came alongside to sample the salted pork bits tossed to them. The big birds would be lifted to the deck, fed pork and turned loose. The captain and mate caught an albatross which they killed and dressed and ordered the cook to prepare it for dinner the next day, but during the night somebody tossed it over the side. Some of the men were superstitious and had heard albatross brought good luck and should not be killed.

July 4 arrived when the ship was in the midst of an Antarctic winter. It was celebrated by "fireworks," two fights between the bos'n and the Greek, Angelo Varellas. They rolled on the slippery deck, neither getting in a solid blow and neither appeared hurt.

That day the cook went to bed with severe abdominal pains, diagnosed by the inexperienced crew as either a rupture or appendicitis. Later, it was determined he had been hit hard by a flying stove lid when the ship rolled. He was bedridden for most of the remainder of the trip and others took over the galley. Angelo Varellas proved to be the best substitute cook, making tasty concoctions from a limited supply of foods. He used ample portions of spices and garlic to improve the fare.

Ordinary Seaman Rowley went to bed with a sprained ankle, but feigned appendicitis. Other crew members popped into his room to find him reading a magazine, which he hastily put aside and complained of pains. The bos'n finally called his act and ordered him to get back to work or lose his union card. Rowley was back on the job with his next watch, looking a bit sheepish and very quiet.

Ira Cheney was hospitalized a second time when a jibing sail boom swung around very fast, mowing down four men. Cheney was the only one badly hurt. At one time, four members of the crew were laid up, forcing the rest of the crew to work harder and longer hours than normally. The work was made difficult by the port list caused by the shifted deckload. This was relieved in the South Atlantic when a storm pounded most of it back and the vessel resumed an even keel.

As the *Tango* drew closer to Cape Town, it ran without lights at night because the diesel generator was shut down to eliminate a tell-tale signal transmitted many miles under water. The captain feared the sound might attract an enemy submarine or raider.

An inspection of lifeboats revealed they were in unseaworthy condition. Fred Bitte undertook repairs, bending on thin sheets of steel over weak and rusted spots and soldering them in place. Then he applied a coat of cement inside the bottoms, hoping this would keep the boats afloat in case they were needed. *Tango* was in dangerous territory.

During the final days of the voyage the men cleaned themselves, washed their clothing, discarded winter underwear, and shaved off their beards. They slept in their clothes and carried their personal papers in their pockets to have them in case of a hurried evacuation of the vessel. Emergency supplies were sacked ready for the lifeboats.

Finally, *Tango* arrived off Cape Town August 16 and was towed in to an anchorage, much to the relief of the crew. The disappointing thing about it was that they were not expected, no shipping agent met them, no money was ready for pay-off for those who wanted shore leave, and they were not allowed to go ashore for two days.

This crew had been out at sea for 105 days and nearly 15,000 miles without sighting another ship or a bit of land until the final day, when a slow plodding Liberty appeared astern. It caused some consternation among the men, who feared it might be a sea-raider or a submarine on the prowl. But *Tango* ran away from the other vessel when a strong favorable wind came up.

Tango averaged about six miles an hour from the Columbia River—not bad.

This has been a brief summary of the voyage from the viewpoints of two crew members. Now, let them tell their story in detail, first Archie McPhee's daily logs, followed by Fred Bitte's diary notes, as originally written during the voyage.

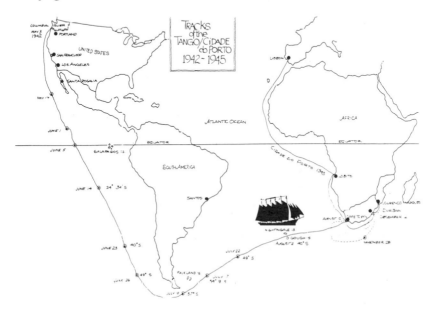

Chapter 6

South to the Gay Twenties

Log by Archie McPhee and Diary of Fred Bitte.

A. McPhee's Folly

Time April 28, 1942
Place: Aboard the S.V. Tango

Leading Characters

Carl D. Gundersen, Captain
Peter Holt, Chief Mate
Jimmy Burke, 2nd Mate and Bos'n
Hans Moller, A.B.
George St. Clair, A.B. and delegate
Howard Jones, A.B.
Angelo Varellas, A.B. (Later, "The Greek")
Charles Carlson, A.B., W.P. (Watch Partner)
Chuck Hammer, A.B., W.P.
Joe Kaplan, A.B., W.P. (Later, "The Jew")
Archibald D. McPhee, A.B., W.P.
Ira Cheney, O.S., W.P.
Mural Lee Rowley, O.S.
Gene Luce, Sparks (Radioman)
Charles LeMon, Cook
Bill Hahn, Messboy
Fred Bitte, Donkeyman and Carpenter

April 28, 1942

Signed on at Shipping Commissioner's, 10 a.m. Aboard ship, 4 p.m.

April 29

McPhee—Securing gear and having newspaper pictures taken. Left dock at 11 a.m. for Astoria—power, two tugs. Arrived Astoria, 5:10 p.m.

April 30

Quite a curiosity for Astoria fishermen. Hailed a large Coast Guard boat whose crew had come out sightseeing; invited them aboard for coffee. To my surprise they accepted.

May 1

Still at anchor. Cannot get cook. Radio operator flying from New York. (Ed.—He came by bus from Seattle.)

May 2

One W.P. (watch partner), Carlson, still on a big wine drunk. Everybody peeved because we can't go ashore.

May 3

McPhee—Radio operator arrived, also cook. Angelo's cousin, an Astoria fisherman, came alongside and gave us a couple of nice sturgeon, then went ashore to get the fellows some whiskey. Coast Guard saw him bring it aboard. Big investigation. Weighed anchor—lots of sightseers—escort by two C.G. boats and pilot boat—two newspaper cameramen aboard—towed about two miles past lightship. Got all but two sails up when the pilot boat went back, taking the cameramen. They felt bad as they wanted to get us under full sail.

Waited for this day for six weeks—quite a thrill. The wheel is on the poop deck and has no house. It sure is going to be a picnic to get back on a steamship.

May 4

Bitte—May 4 to 25 (no diary during interim). Working south and farther to sea, getting warmer with hard tropical rains. My ceiling leaks. I could take a shower in my room. We fear an equatorial calm and long stay.

May 5

McPhee—Making about one knot. The slower we go the more money we make. There are about 8 blackfish playing around our ship. They have halitosis. Besides the escort of whales we have about 100 goonies following us.

May 6

Making one to five knots. Thousands of Portuguese Men-O-War over the waves.

May 7

McPhee—Wind picking up—5 to 7½ knots today. Had to reef in the driver and lost my watch doing so. First day the cook hasn't fed the fishes. Messboy is sick and wants to get off at Pedro. Donkeyman says he is sick and wants to get off, also. Lost our whales, but still have the goonies and thousands of Men-of-War.

May 8

McPhee—Red letter day, made 12 knots for two hours and averaged about seven all day. Rained, so I got a bucket of water for a bath. Going to let my whiskers grow, saves water and blades. My W.P.s supply me with a number of laughs. Kaplan is a Jew, the other two are Swedes. Kaplan's references to money matters irks them considerably. They bicker back and forth trying to use me as a balance. If I take sides it will be with the Jew. Everyone is giving him a tough time.

May 9

McPhee—Tough day. Fellow next to me on the foot ropes of the jib slipped and slid into my leg, wrenching my knee. Made a mile in three minutes and 22 seconds, averaging about 11 knots. (Sic) (Editor's note—There must have been a misunderstanding of the time, which would have resulted in a speed of 17.8 knots. At 11 knots, the time would be 5 minutes and 27 seconds.)

May 10

McPhee—Made 66 miles in the last six hours. Lots of trouble today—messboy has become insubordinate. Captain told him if he didn't snap out of it he would go in the brig. Steward has turned out to be a bum cook and union man—doesn't want to put out a night lunch, and doesn't want us to use the galley at night. We'll fix that even if someone has to have a sore head. "It's a Hell Ship, Ma!"

May 11

McPhee—Cook made statement: "Captain's orders were not to use galley at night." After about 15 minutes of arguing, I figured he was lying and asked him to go with me to the captain. After a little bluffing he admitted he was lying. So I gave him a good bawling out. He finally told me to lay off because he was a ju jitsu expert and he would fix me. So I reefed in his sails a bit. Having a meeting tomorrow—hot session? Off the Mexican Coast now. It took the *Star of Scotland*, a sailing vessel of the same rig as ours, 21 days to do what we have done in seven. She is about two months ahead of us. Only making about 2 knots and might have to change to port tack. Had two buckets of rain water, so I took a bath and washed clothes—a real luxury. Two baths in a week.

May 12

McPhee—Meeting was a torrid session—developed a little hard feeling between the two watches. Because the Jew puts something up, they talk it down even if he is right. A man off their watch is delegate and another is chairman. We will have to rearrange that to give us more power. Have started working out. Coupled with pulling rope, it makes a pretty strenuous day. I can go the farthest up the shrouds. Made about a dollar a mile today—in other words, we are going quite slow.

May 13

McPhee—In tuna water—spent a little time rigging up some fishing lines today. Ran around deck in just a pair of shorts, obtained a good start for a suntan. If the friction aboard this ship gets much worse there is going to be a lot of trouble this trip. Cheney is now being accused of carrying tales to the Captain—crew takes such things quite serious. I now have the radio operator and Cheney working out with me.

May 14

McPhee—Cook has turned out to be just a pantryman and pastry cook, and we can't live on just cakes and pies. Kaplan, the Jew boy, is on the agitator type and when he actually has something to holler about he really goes to town. He has been giving the cook so much hell that the cook threatened him with a cleaver, which called for another meeting. There is talk of demoting him to O.S. and make him work on deck and put someone else in the galley. Went up on the foremast to grease the heel of the claw. After I finished I went up to the truck and shimmed across the main brace to the mainmast instead of climbing up the mainmast. The Captain saw me and threw a fit. Bawled me and the Bos'n out. Got out in the sun about five hours today and got a sunburn. Saw a few sunfish in the water. It is hard on the eyes to watch them. Making about 3 knots.

May 15

McPhee—Have started drinking coffee because the water is not tasting right. Had some lousy spaghetti today. The spaghetti Hilts and I made was ten times as good. This sailing ship work is cutting my waistline down. I have also quit eating potatoes, and instead of bread I eat hardtack. You see, I don't want to get fat like Tom Fleming—ha-ha. Hit the N.E. trades today, so have changed to starboard tack. Making about 5 knots.

May 16
McPhee—Rationing of water started today. Will remain such until a couple of heavy rains. About eight of us have shaved our heads, including myself. They also took the hot water tank out of the galley to save water. Cloudy, cold weather, which is hard on my suntan. Making about 6 knots.

May 17
McPhee—Hard to get sleep—sleeping hours are different each day. On 6, off 6, on 4, off 4, on 4, off 6, on 6, off 4, etc. Making about 8½ knots. Keep getting the breaks and we will make the trip in 90 days. This is such a hungry ship we have lost all the goonies except one. We thought we had lost him when we had chicken for dinner, but a check-up proved it to be real chicken. We were abeam of Cape San Lucas, which is on the point of Lower California. We will go past the Galapagos Islands on the west and then come in close to shore, according to the Captain. Navy's orders.

May 18
McPhee—Sea and wind picking up. Have been running about 9½ knots. Never a dull moment today. Joe, the Jew, refused to sew canvas this A.M. because the palms are partly pigskin. I was the last one to dinner today because I had the last wheel. When I got to the table all the fried potatoes were gone, so the cook asked me if a big piece of salt pork out of the pot of lima beans would be an acceptable substitute. Joe was at halfmast with a spoon of beans at the time and had already eaten some. He thought the cook was trying to pull a fast one on him because he hadn't told him there was pork in the beans. We had to break them up and watch them closely. Two-thirds of our meat supply is pork so it looks like Joe is going to have a tough time. Have been playing a lot of cribbage lately but I will have to display a little more brains at it.

May 19

Clearing up, making an average of 4½ knots. Making sennets today reminds me of working for Francis on pompoms.

May 20

McPhee—Cool and cloudy which is quite a break. The sun was directly overhead yesterday and we should have had some hot weather, but the temp. is running around 80 degrees. More trouble is looming. Sailors are supposed to take orders from the bos'n, not the mate. Port watch has been handshaking with the mate and decided to take orders from him instead of the bos'n. Being on the mate's watch he gives them the pick of the jobs. We are getting all the dirty jobs and are going to see things are changed. Threw buckets of salt water at each other today for baths. Ran into some big swells last night, caused by shoal water depth that ran from 2,000 fathoms to 76 fathoms inside of a mile or so.

May 21

McPhee—What a beautiful night. Exceptionally clear with a brilliant half moon shedding its silvery light, combined with a ship under full sail. Romance and adventure on the high seas. Big meeting tonight and it is going to be packed with hard feelings. Getting on a salt meat diet—all fresh meats and fruits are gone.

May 22

McPhee—Had a meeting that came out in our favor. Another meeting tomorrow to do something about the cooking, which is lousy. Another unusually beautiful night. These beautiful nights recall memories of our friends and dear ones at home. The privilege of using the word "home" and knowing it is an asset of ours at a time of use is really something. You also realize this when "from home you roam." Your biggest comfort and anticipation bring your thoughts of return. Idle patter. Slacked off the sheets at 10:20 p.m., picking up another knot. Doing about 8.

May 23

McPhee—Saw a few tuna and bonita but didn't catch any. Had a meeting but didn't accomplish anything. If a fellow can't cook, a meeting won't improve his cooking. He tries hard and isn't a bit lazy and might improve with practice. It is tough being a guinea pig some days, though. Making 8 knots today. The 2nd mate has been talking to me lately about going pearling after the war. He has a couple of good spots in mind and figures $2,500 apiece would get a good two-masted schooner, two diving outfits, a couple of years provisions, and leave about $1,500 to run on. Calls for a lot of thinking, though.

May 24

McPhee—Becalmed, three-fourths moon. Nights of tropical splendor. Had canned chicken for dinner. It was almost as good as Hilts and I fried up in the mountains. Standing joke aboard ship: "Captain, someone called the cook an s.o.b." "Well, I want to know who called the s.o.b. a cook." All I wear now is a pair of shorts and sandals. Sure saves on washing.

May 25

McPhee—Becalmed from about 10:50 to 12:20 when a rain squall hit us and we made about 6 knots. I got a bar of soap and took a good bath and then washed my clothes in the rain.

May 26

McPhee—Typical tropical weather today, rained about 10 hours. We got more fresh water than we know what to do with. All tanks and miscellaneous containers are full. The Greek has a touch of fever every time he gets back into the tropics. Worked four hours in the rain in shorts. Reeling off about 8 knots. Barometer is falling. If it falls much farther we will have to reef the sails. All the earmarks of a blow.

May 27

McPhee—Logging about 2 knots. Rained more in last 12 hours than it rains in a month of Portland's rainy season. Had to jibe over three times on first watch and twice on second watch. Quarters leak pretty bad. Going to try to hook the company for some new clothes when we get to port.

May 28

McPhee—The Jew and I sewed a leech line around the rain catcher this morning and one of the port watch made a crack to the mate about it being a bum job. So the Jew caught him on deck after dinner and worked him over. The fellow was Moller. He is about 6'3" and weighs about 210. The Jew is about 5'9" and weighs about 175. The Jew knocked the Swede down three times and was knocked down once himself. About a 28 deg. list to deck hindered both men. Adverse winds, had to steer E. by N. most of the day—headed back to Portland. Lots of flying fish.

May 29

McPhee—Four hundred miles from the Equator. In the bad doldrum area, which is 5 deg. either side of the Equator. Rained 16 hours of the last 24, and when it rains it really comes down. Had a meeting—the other watch pays the Jew more respect since the fight. The meeting went our way. Stood under one of the sails and had a shower. The sails catch a lot of rain and it comes down on you like a fire hose—some fun. Logging about 1½ knots.

May 30

McPhee—Quite a few bonita around the bow. With four lines out the only result was the loss of three plugs. Won seven games of crib today. Holiday so we had chicken dinner. Logging about 4.

Bitte—We are now 6 deg. above the Equator. A year ago today we went to the beach and had a swell time with the family.

May 31

McPhee—Saw springers, porpoises and bonita today, but nobody caught anything. Got the tail end of a blow about 6 p.m. and had to take in the flying jib. Cleared up at 8 and it turned out to be a nice night with a full moon. Wind is still unfavorable. Have to steer E. by S. when our course should be SSE. 270 miles from Equator. Made only 130 miles in 3½ days.

Bitte—Sunday, Sparks and I made a little wager that the one losing the most games of rummy between here and our first shore leave buys the winner all the malted milks he can drink at one sitting. Am one game to the good. Come on ye old rabbit's foot, do your stuff.

June 1

McPhee—Steering ENE, seven points off our course. Weather is contrary to all charts, has the Captain and mate puzzled. We are afraid of a typhoon. Sparks got a message from another ship saying they were being chased by another vessel thought to be a raider. We have an awfully poor ship's radio. Can receive and transmit only 500 miles, so that ship was within 500 miles of us.

June 2

McPhee—Changed to port tack, steering SSW and making better time. Had three glasses of prune juice for breakfast. It proved itself more thorough than castor oil.

June 3

McPhee—Little excitement—a little diesel motor used for the pumps and lights in port, which is next to our room, caught fire in its wiring. Smoke was coming out of the foc'sle and one of the fellows on the other watch woke us up with yells of "fire." It looked like the fire was in the Jew's locker.

He almost went nuts, throwing his clothes out of the locker, especially his two suits and an overcoat which he says were damaged by smoke and the company has to pay him $150. Hit the SE trades today, are making about 6 knots which is pretty good when we are supposed to be in the doldrums. Expect to cross the Equator tomorrow.

Bitte—Nearing the Equator. I wish the little lady and the boys could be here to share these wonderful tropic nights with me.

June 4

McPhee—Coolest weather I have seen in the tropics. Have to sleep with a sheet and spread over me at night. Quite a break, though, for on this ship we have no fans and the quarters are small with four men to the room. Will cross the Equator about 1 a.m.

June 5

McPhee—Passed the Equator but there isn't enough friendly spirit and good will among the fellows to hold a King Neptune's Court. This is customary on ships crossing the Equator and the object is to initiate those whose first crossing it happens to be. Had a meeting today, recalled the delegate, elected the Jew in his place. Gives us more power. The Jew will do anything the bos'n and I tell him. Asked the messboy and cook to pool their wages between them and split the work because the cook can't cook, but he can bake. The messboy can cook but he can't bake. Kind of a Jack Sprat affair. 'Twixt the two of them they ought to do pretty keen. Asked the cook about the disappearance of the toaster. He finally admitted he threw it over the side one night to get even with us after we had beefed about a supper. Captain is going to log him for that.

Bitte—Crossed the Equator at 9 this morning. Little less than 33 days from the Columbia River. Considered good time. Sparks is 2 games up on me.

June 6
McPhee—Messboy refuses to help with the cooking. Says he won't work more than 8 hours a day. Rest of us are on a 12-hour day. There was a school of albacore around the ship all day. With nine lines out we couldn't catch one. Then we made three harpoons and still no fish were gotten. Chips has a motion picture camera and had a time picturing our futile efforts. Very little wind, logging only about 2 knots and sometimes less.

June 7
McPhee—Had some traditional sailing sport today. Had a bos'n chair over the end of the bowsprit. Ship was making about 5 knots. Every time she pitched she would dunk us in the water and when she raised her bow we would swing out. Coming in we would go in the water and it looked like the ship would hit us when the slack came out of the rope and we would bounce and skip over the waves. Sparks, Cheney and I were the only ones who went over. Chips took motion pictures of us. Out of the doldrums, we are 347 miles south of the Equator at noon.

Bitte—Sunday. Five weeks out and still trouble with the generator. Took pictures of the boys fishing and taking baths swinging in a bos'n chair from the bowsprit. We are 1,100 miles from shore.

June 8
McPhee—Sails are getting a little baggy; took in on all the peak halyards this a.m. It left the leeches taut but the sails were slack by the leeches. Looks like some work on the sails when we get to port. On a port tack it is hard to stay in our bunks. Had an unusually heavy list this a.m. and I would roll out onto the floor. Upper bunk—only damage was a sprained thumb. Heavy wind, making about 7½ knots.

June 9

McPhee—Heavy weather, shipping seas over the bow and have about a 28-degree list. Had to take in the flying jib, take a reef in the driver and take in all the sheets. The hour previous to doing this I was on lookout and took a good workout. With the work on the sails I was a tired boy. No more workouts in heavy weather. Might have to take in the driver completely. There is an eight-inch rip in it.

June 10

McPhee—Cleared up so sails were back up. At 5:45 a storm hit and we are really in it now. Had to take in the flying jib. Three clamps by a shipping board splice by the martingale came together making some slack in the bowsprit. The bowsprit jerking up and down broke the peak halyard on the outer jib. It was a real job taking it in. The wind was whipping the sail around and we were shipping heavy weather sprays over the bowsprit. Got all wet and a little bruised. Wish Chips had taken some pictures of that. Next, the driver had to come in. That was comparatively easy, though. Clamps have slipped on the shrouds of the mainmast and there is a kink in the top of the foremast. "Romance and adventure on the high seas." I won't have to work out tonight.

June 11

McPhee—Cleared up, spent most of the day tightening up on rigging. Couldn't get the kink out of the foremast. It really looks bad. Most of the throat halyards are not led properly and they are badly chafed. If one of them chafed through there would be hell to pay for a while. Captain is getting a little nasty. We had been working from 12 to 1 just a few days ago when we noticed in our contract no work other than work pertaining to safety of the vessel to be done during the noon hour. He keeps finding penny ante jobs, claiming they are essential work and working us after hours. He will lose in the long run 'cause we are going to install a slowdown program. Cook ruined a chicken dinner today. The chicken comes canned and ready cooked, but he puts it in a pot and boils it anyway, cooks the meat from the bones and puts it on the table looking like a soup. Each person, as he took his helping, did a little beefing and growling at the cook. The cook finally got so mad he went to the Captain and the Captain bawled him out. He made the statement that if we didn't lay off he was going to jump overboard. He is crazy enough to do it. Sample: He has been married three times. First time he was 24, she was 40 with five children. Paying her $50 a month alimony. Second time he was 27, she 35 with two children. Paying her $25 a month alimony. Third time he was 32 and she was 34 with two children and bore him one. Pays her $75 a month. He has to pay more alimony than the average man makes a month. Was in jail for failure to pay alimony and was released just to take this job. After a sample like that, don't you think he might jump overboard? If I were him I'd do it just to gyp those old hens out of the alimony.

Bitte—15 deg. below the Equator. I'm five games ahead of Sparks. May drink on him if luck holds.

June 12

McPhee—Captain waited until the noon hour and then wanted the driver and outer jib raised. Pretty small minded of him and the crew resents it. He can do this legally if necessary for safety of navigation of the ship. But we were just puttering around all a.m. In fact, he had us scraping the roof over the heads of the watch below. When they complained it kept them awake, he told them he was running the ship and his orders were law. As soon as it is time for them to get up he takes us away from there and has the sails raised.

Had a meeting and Cheney was barred because he carries everything to the skipper. Cheney feels he is a little better than the rest of us because: 1. His father was a sea captain. 2. Donald F. McKay, the famous builder of sailing ships (clippers), was his great uncle. Through his father I believe he has gotten a little dislike for unions, which all captains have. He would have preferred going to a maritime school but he has weak eyes. If he doesn't straighten out he will not be able to get into the union. Then his only way to sea will be as a passenger. That will be hard on him for he really has a love for the sea. The Southern Cross is almost overhead tonight. We are about 1,100 miles south of the Equator and about 1,500 miles off shore. Picked up some gulls today, figure they must be from Tahiti. Logging about 8.

June 13

McPhee—Saw lots of flying fish today. Almost halfway in 42 sailing days, which is unusually good time. We have passed the slowest stretch which is in the doldrums. If we do not strike any bad weather we should make it in less than 100 days. Gets dark at 5:30 and is getting noticeably colder at night. Logging around 5 today.

Bitte—Now 21 deg., 36 min. south at noon and going SxE after going SxW for some time. Six games ahead. Raining a little, may not have to ration water.

June 14

McPhee—Cook baked a cake and set it out to cool. Someone swiped the cake. Aroused the cook's ire and he began denouncing sailors and branding us thieves, etc. Sailors then began telling him what a lousy cook he was and said they were going to run him off the ship at Cape Town. A couple of fights were barely averted. The cook made the statement he would jump over the side then and there, but he was writing a book and wanted to finish it first. The wind shifted on us several times, making us work Sunday—tch! tch! Making from 2 to 5 knots and steering SExS.

Bitte—Sunday. Six weeks from the Columbia. We are at 24 deg., 34 min. south, 1,000 miles from shore. About one-half way to Africa. Ate last cookie, some candy left.

Chapter 7

The Roaring Forties and Howling Fifties

June 15

McPhee—Could write a book on what happened the last two days. Didn't have a chance to make this entry until a day late. The Jew is a labor fanatic and aspires to be a labor leader; his idol is Harry Bridges. To further himself in this direction he is continually striving to improve conditions and buck the shipowners. His song is as follows:

The Internationale

Arise, you prisoners of starvation!
Arise, you wretched of the earth,
For justice thunders condemnation,
A better world's in birth.
No more traditions chains shall bind us.
Arise, you slaves, no more in thrall!
The earth shall rise on new foundations,
We have been naught; we shall be all.

Chorus

'Tis the final conflict,
Let each stand in his place,
The Internationale shall be the Human race!
'Tis the final conflict,
Let each stand in his place;
The Internationale shall be the Human race!

I have just asked for a statement: "An international labor union would mean the end of all wars, and any disputes between capital and industries would have to be settled without using the laboring man as a pawn. Living would be standardized and the majority of human suffering would be done away with.—Joe Kaplan."

He is a member of the Young Communists League. His happier moments are when he is "straightening out" a captain or mate. Since we have made him delegate he has been pestering the life out of the captain and mate and also getting results. He was all wound up over something that was "phony" and made the statement he would have the captain put in jail when we got to Cape Town. This got back to the Captain. Kind of scared him, too, and also made him mad. Second mate told the Jew. The Jew then favored for diplomatic reasons to try and square things with the Captain, which he did.

About two hours later the cook was overheard complaining to the mate about the crew squawking about dinner. The mate's reply was, if we continued squawking he would give the cook something to put in our grub that would shut us up. This almost started a riot. There were threats made to kill if this was carried out. The delegate, roused to a terrible rage, went to the Captain and threatened to have the mate put in jail and his license taken away. He left the Captain cursing and talking to himself, walking up and down the bridge. Had humorous aspects.

During the night the halyard to the outer jib carried away. After dinner we fixed this and set the sail again, greased the heels and claws aloft. Hammer took three masts and I took three.

The barometer dropped about 20 deg. and we were in for a blow. Lowered outer jib which we had just finished raising, took in the driver and then the storm hit us. It was raising hell with the sails and we had to jibe over. While jibing over, the mizzen got away from us and jumped her cleat. Everyone jumped clear but Cheney, he still clinging to the hauling part. It pulled him almost to the block and whipped him out over the side. As he came back the wind caught it again, gave it an awful jerk whipping Cheney up into the air about 15 feet. He came down on his head and arms. He has a broken nose and can't use either of his arms.

A couple of us ran to help and the Captain hollered "Leave him alone—he's all right. Let him lay there and take care of the sails." The lee rail was under water just like those pictures you see of yacht racing. We were shipping water over the weather side and it was raining heavily and the wind was blowing about 40 knots. All this made working conditions extremely bad. The Captain was running around shouting orders and cursing us in Norwegian and English—damned provoking and disgusting. I am still mad about it two days later.

Had to take in the jigger. While putting relieving tackle on the booms to keep them from jerking back and forth, I had a thrill. I had to go up on the boom of the mizzen mast to hook the block of the relieving tackle in a strap. While I was hooking it up a gust of wind caught the sail from the lee side and bellied her to the side I was sitting on, knocking me off the boom. I was hanging onto a lazy jack, though, and just took a nice swing through the air. Didn't have a chance to eat until 7 o'clock and had worked up an appetite. Rained hard all night and it was hard telling how fast we were going.

Bitte—About 26 deg. south and 1,000 miles west of South America. Ordinary seaman on starboard watch was drawn aloft by line and fell on deck, face, hands, back, sprained wrist.

June 16

McPhee—Cleared up and we were becalmed until about 6 p.m. Saw a lot of shark but they wouldn't take any hooks. Cheney spent a pretty bad night, his arms pained him quite a bit. Opinions vary as to whether his arms are broken or just sprained. There isn't a good first aid man aboard.

Bitte—Becalmed today and no sun so we didn't get our location. It is getting noticeably colder now and we will have to get out heavier clothing right soon. Seems quite odd for it to be getting cooler at a time of year when I am accustomed to seeing hot weather approaching. Broke even with Sparks at rummy so am still 6 games ahead.

June 17

McPhee—Barometer is still acting up so the Captain has left the sails down that we took in Monday. Picked up four albatross which are nicely marked. They are all white underneath except a black fringe around the winds and black wing tips. Tops of their bodies are white with black skull caps; tip of tail is black, wings on top are black with white fringe around the edge and white tips. The bos'n and Captain made a trap, caught one and killed it. This, I did not like. The Captain took the feet, which he is going to make into a tobacco pouch and the head he is going to make into an inkwell. The head, he said, would be worth at least $50. The bird has a ten-foot wingspread which is considered small. The Captain ordered the cook to prepare it for dinner tomorrow. I shall not eat any. They are the only living things you see at sea outside of fish, and I thought there was a tradition against killing them. We haven't seen a ship since we left Astoria, and to have these birds soaring around the ship is just like having company. Didn't eat much today—codfish for breakfast, dinner and supper. The Captain is making out the menus now and prefers codfish to turkey and can't understand why some of the rest of us don't. Next time this happens I am going to refuse to work until I can get something I can eat. Logging about 5 knots with sails down.

Bitte—Clear today with light winds this morning. Fired up the steam plant to raise the sails we dropped during the squall two days ago, but the wind came up in the meantime so the sails are still down. May try again tomorrow. Were 30 deg. south at noon today. I am in Sparks' room listening to an American radio program while I am writing this.

June 18

McPhee—Set the driver, the jigger and the outer jib. The only sail now down is the flying jib. Kicked about the food today and the Captain said we were eating too good and he was going to feed us more rice and beans. There is 600 pounds of rice and 1,000 pounds of beans aboard, and also 113 sacks of flour. According to the Captain this is to make up the bulk of our diet. We are 32 deg. below the Equator now and it is getting cold enough for some of the fellows to put on their underwear, about 42 degrees.

Bitte—We raised the sails today. Wish they had a good electric winch on this ship. Would make it much less trouble getting the darned sails up. Only reached the 32 deg. today, fell a little under. Some of the fellows caught an albatross yesterday. It seems they use the hide for making purses and stuff. Sparks beat me two games in a row tonight and cut my lead to five games. Boy, is he hot.

June 19

McPhee—Big mystery of the South Pacific is who threw the albatross overboard early this a.m. after the Captain and mate had spent an hour picking and cleaning it. Foresail, which is right over the foc'sle, came down about 3:20 this morning. Sounded like the whole mast gave way. Didn't waste much time getting out on deck. A shackle had broken and dropped a double block. The rigging aboard is not very well laid out. We are going to have lots of trouble with it. A small squall hit us at 4:10 p.m. and we had to lower the driver and change to port tack. With Cheney laid up with his arms and one man at the wheel, there are only three of us to do the work on our watch. It makes a lot of difference when you are pulling on the sheets. Having one man short means more lookouts and wheel turns, also. Had salt bacon for breakfast along with hotcakes, bean soup and pork and beans for dinner, fried salt pork, potatoes, spinach and gravy made from salt pork. After my supper I drank a glass of water and the whole meal came up. This made me good and mad because I had worked hard today and was hungry. So I went to the Captain and told him I would not stand my watch tonight if I did not get something else to eat. We settled on three eggs and some tomato juice. Then the Jew, who doesn't eat pork, came off the wheel seeing pork for supper and he flew into a rage and went to the Captain demanding something else to eat. He settled for a pound can of roast beef. Steering SxE and logging about 4.

Bitte—The first sail to work loose and come down by itself did this morning at 4 o'clock. Boy, what a racket. Thought the ship was falling apart. So I had to get up steam again today to raise it. I didn't hear where we were today— somewhere in the South Pacific no doubt. Haven't put on my heavy underwear yet, it's too hot in the boiler room, but on deck it is regular November weather. Seven games up on Sparks now. Got hopes of final victory.

June 20

McPhee—Wind picked up so much our lee rail was in the water, calling for all hands at 10 o'clock, just when our watch had turned in. Lowered the jigger, spanker, inner jib and outer jib. We were doing about 14 for a while on a SES course. We are now 40 deg. south. Only 15 deg. farther south is the latitude of Cape Horn, but we are also about 1,000 miles west of it. Expect to be around the Horn about the 4th of July, which will be in the dead of winter. This water is by far the most phosphorescent I have seen. Just happened to think last week was the Rose Festival, and also the cherries in our back yard should be ripe, and here I am wearing winter underwear.

Bitte—We are down here where the wind really blows. Only three sails up and we are moving as fast as we have any time on the trip. Hope it don't blow any harder before morning. Would hate to have to lower a sail in the middle of the night. Am running the Delco plant nights now. Makes it nice to have lights but it makes me extra work. Am seven games up on Sparks but he is ahead in the game we are now playing.

June 21

McPhee—Feeling sorry for myself. Had every kind of squall imaginable—rain, hail, sleet and combinations of them. Had to take in the main sail during a snow storm with the Captain running around like a maniac. Out of the ten sails we have only three up—the mainsail jib, the fore sail, and the mizzen. Strong winds and heavy seas. Every time the ship rolls the lee rail goes under and when she comes back she ships a sea over the weather side. When she takes a bad pitch she takes a big one over the bow. When you are on the lookout, which is on the foc'sle head at the bow, you get water from both sides, the front and the skies. When you are at the wheel you are without any shelter at all and have to steer from the weather side. Every time the sea hits the rudder the wheel gives an awful yank on your arms. The door to our foc'sle isn't watertight and there are three leaks in the roof over my bunk. We had salt ham twice today and my oilskins leak. Now, don't you feel sorry for me. PS—they are running the light plant all night now in case of emergency. The plant is next to our foc'sle, keeps our room full of fumes and we can't have any doors or port holes open or we would be flooded out. We lowered the main sail with only our watch and are short one man. Whenever there is a sail to lower on the other watch, the mate calls for all hands, breaking up what little sleep we do get. Making 7 and 8 with only three sails up gives you an idea of the force of the wind.

Bitte—Below 40 deg. south now. We lowered one more sail today and have only two sails up now, besides one jib. It is getting colder every day and we can expect freezing weather by the first of July. We may have chance of seeing snowballs in July, yet. Hope not too many. Today is Father's Day by the calendar—one Hell of a place for a father to be, on a ship miles from home. Wonder how the wife and boys are making it. Will be glad to hear from them when we get to Africa.

June 22

McPhee—Clearing up, moon and stars out tonight. Sea is still heavy and winds strong, but the barometer is rising. Carlson opened our door today and shipped a couple of big seas and we're flooded out. Hell of a mess. The Jew damned near went nuts. Ate eight eggs for breakfast. There are only enough for one or two more meals. Canned milk is almost gone. Also running out of coffee, out of chicken, onions have all rotted, two of the sacks of sugar left had kerosene spilled on them, and the cook has started to feed us salt cabbage which is lousy. Making about 5 knots.

Bitte—The wind is still blowing today but the barometer is rising so we may have to let up soon. If we do I'll have to fire up again to lower sails and get in shape for a real blow as we are getting into the middle of winter now. About 43 deg. south now and getting colder every day. Sparks had held me at rummy, winning as often as he is losing. I have a point lead on him now.

June 23

McPhee—On deck from 4 a.m. to 6 p.m. today. Lowered the foresail and put a double reef in it, then raised. Put a single reef in the main sail and raised it. Lowered the mizzen and put a single reef in it and set it. Put a double reef in the spanker and set it. Jibed over to port tack. Now have four sails and a jib set, logging about 7 knots. Picked up some more albatross and some other birds about one-fifth size of the albatross and marked similar except at the top of their wings which are black and white designs and heads all black. Had some lousy barreled salt beef for dinner and supper today. For every pound that is eaten 20 pounds go over the side. I wish my fat friend, T.V.F., could see my waistline now, a slim 32½ compared with his probably 42½.

Bitte—Got up steam today and the boys reefed and raised three sails today. It was quite a nice day but the wind is coming up again this evening. We are having headwinds and aren't

94

progressing as fast as we hoped to. Sparks and I are still holding even at rummy, with me still in the lead.

June 24

McPhee—Ran into a blow at 8 this morning. All hands were called to lower the mizzen. The sea and wind were abeam and we shipped some pretty big seas. By noon we were becalmed, the sun was shining and the world didn't seem such a bad place after all. It is a nice night with the moon shining and the stars out. Have a fair wind and doing about 3 knots.

Bitte—Rained today, dropped the mizzen and changed tack this afternoon. We are headed straight for the Horn, which they figure is still 1,800 miles away so it will be 10 or 12 days before we can hope to reach it if we have fair sailing weather.

June 25

McPhee—Cold moonlight night with a heavy wind and large swells. Steering E½N, logging about 6. One of the lifeboats, which are metal, was badly dented by a sea Sunday. We put a fence of 4 by 10's on the outboard sides to protect them. Something is wrong with the steering compass. It varies from 2½ to 4 points with the standard compass. Lousy stinking codfish for two meals today.

Bitte—We had a very nice day today. It was cool but the sun shone most of the time and that tends to make things a little cheery even when it is quite cold. If the weather is good tomorrow we may raise another sail to speed things up a bit. We haven't been doing so well since the wind let up. Boy, I hope we make it around the Horn without experiencing a real blow. These squalls make the ship bounce around bad enough.

June 26

McPhee—ExN, logging up to 9. Full moon and not as cold. Captain told us to keep a more careful lookout; we are in danger of running across icebergs. We are now 49 deg. south and about 700 miles off shore. Have a month of winter ahead of us and the worst time of year to go around the Horn. It looks like a four-month trip now. We still have 6,000 miles to go and will go farther figuring our tacks. Rowley, the O.S. on the port watch, got a little off course today and the sails started flapping. The Captain bawled him out, calling him everything in the book, both in English and Norwegian. Rowley sassed him aback and the Captain squared off and threatened to hit him. They will have a hard time to get a crew for the next trip if they keep this captain. Ran into some mountainous seas from 8 to 12 this a.m., and the ship was awash most of the time.

Bitte—Rough and windy today. Little off my feed but not feeling too bad for the weather we are riding. We are less than 1,000 miles from the Horn from what I heard if any stock can be put in it. Most anything can be heard on this ship. Most of the doors have swelled up so I am pretty busy whittling them down to fit the holes. Sparks has whittled my lead at rummy down to five games, bless his little hide. You have to know the little cuss to appreciate that.

June 27

McPhee—Pretty full moon rose right in front of us. We were heading E½N. St. Clair got hit by a sea last night. It knocked him about 15 feet against the spanker, wrenching his knee pretty badly, a bed case. Captain asked the cook for a plate of bacon, didn't like the cuts, so he threw it at the cook, who ducked. Saturday afternoon is supposed to be off except for work necessary for navigation and safety of the ship. The other watch was on deck all a.m. doing general ship's work, then at noon when we start our watch the Captain had us raise the inner jib and the mizzen. Penny ante tactics. It's dark at 4:15 and stays so until about 8 a.m. Logging as much as 9 and made 180 miles in the last 24 hours.

Bitte—Light winds and sea. We hoisted another sail. Today was nice fall weather. It is raining a little this evening. Have been thinking about the boys quite a bit lately. Hope you are making all right with them. Good boys but a lot of life in them and that means work and worry for mother. The peas must be just about full grown now. Wish I was there to work with them, but things didn't work out that way. Maybe different next year, I hope.

June 28

McPhee—Practically becalmed, doing about 2. Unusually mild weather for this part of the world. Cheney got up today. Both of his arms are stiff but the soreness is gone. He is going to stand a couple of lookouts per watch which will help. The little birds following us that resemble albatross in miniature are Cape Horn pigeons. Ate unusually well today— canned Campbell's soup, canned ham, canned orange juice, canned tomatoes, canned peas and the last of the eggs.

Bitte—Sunday, and we have two full months in hope we are getting out of debt. If we aren't I am sure taking this punishment for naught. It is harder than I thought it would be to be away from the family for a few months. It may get easier as time goes on, I hope. We are 1,200 miles from the Horn and practically becalmed. It is about the same as November and early December in Oregon—cold but endurable.

June 29

McPhee—Blow hit us at 12:30. Had to jibe over. Wind was too strong to pull in the sheets so we were raising them over the tackles when the ship came around. Carlson and the Jew each lost control of their tackles and got bad burns on their hands. When they went to the Captain for first aid he blew up, said he had never seen so many accidents on a sailing ship and it had to stop. This went against our grain quite a bit because none of us are trying to get hurt. About 4 a.m. the peak purchase on the spanker broke and dropped the peak. The throat then had to be lowered and gaskets put around the sail—quite a job in heavy weather. Becalmed ever since 9:30 a.m.

Bitte—Lots of wind today. The boys had to drop another sail and we are traveling under three reefed sails and moving right along. The seas are a large way from being calm so my stomach is not doing as well as it could. Things could be worse, though. The boys in the army haven't even got it as comfortable as we have on this ship when they are in action so I guess we haven't much to complain about.

June 30
McPhee—Becalmed until about 10 a.m. Heavy mist and fog. Wind picked up considerably and had shifted by 11, so had to jibe over again. Lost my sou'wester (rain hat) so I made one out of canvas. A good job, too, even if I have to say so.

Bitte—Light winds and rained all day—still is. One man left the sick bay two days ago and another is in with housemaid's knee. Fell over the deckload at night. It is getting warmer as we approach land. Hope to have fair winds and get around the Horn before mid-winter sets in. If it wasn't for the radio this life would be almost unbearable. At least it tells us you folks at home are doing right well as a whole.

July 1
McPhee—What little wind we have has changed to southerly and feels like it is right from the Antarctic. We were working on the poop deck putting up a canvas dodger and the Captain was fishing for albatross from the same. He caught a mollyhook over a cape hen. These are similar to albatross but are more drab in color and have a different beak. We catch them with a V-shaped iron pounded into a piece of wood. The bait is wrapped around the iron which is sharp on the inner edge. All these birds have hooked beaks and when they bite at the meat we jerk the line, catching the beak in the V. When the bird is pulled aboard he is unhurt and not a bit scared. The Captain's bird ate meat off the trap and ate from our hands and posed for pictures. When we ran out of eats, it jumped over the side and flew away. Clear and cold, making about one knot, 780 miles from the Horn.

Bitte—This is our location: S. 52 deg., 8 min.; W. 90 deg., 04 min., which places us about 800 miles from the Horn. It was a nice day, not warm but the sun shone nicely for a few hours. May see the proverbial snowball in July yet. We have been becalmed all day but in this part of the world that may be just the prelude to a hard blow. We have four sails up but they are reefed so they will not have to be dropped too soon in case of a blow. Each day brings us closer to home, even when going away.

July 2

McPhee—Writing this on the morning of the 4th. Reason, a bad storm—on deck 20 hours one stretch. The wind was so heavy it pulled the splice out of the inner jib stay at the mast and dropped the sail over the side. We took in the main, mizzen, spanker and the staysail jib. The only one left up was the foresail and about an hour later the wind ripped it into shreds. We were then without sails but making as much as four knots. Rowley, O.S. on port watch, was hit by a big sea and wrenched his leg. There are now three men laid up and it sure makes more work for the rest of us. Shipping big seas. Man at the wheel was lashed to the worm housing. One sea came out at 4:10. It went clear over the galley and poop deck and raised hell with everything, smashed the lifeboat on the port side, took away the galley stack, came right back in the galley door. Just as the mate started to come out of the saloon door it caught him, knocked him to the floor and all but drowned him. Two or three feet of water in the Captain's quarters which was on the side of the list, drained down below the saloon to the storeroom and ruined flour, macaroni, spaghetti, hardtack and other dried stores. The wind tore the driver and spanker loose from the gaskets we had on them. I never worked so hard in my life, even in a forest fire. Got to go below for 2½ hours but the ship was rolling and pitching so much I was rolled onto the floor four times. Once I was hanging onto the spring and the whole works of us went.

Bitte—Writing this from memory on July 4. On this day, July 2, a stiff wind was blowing. At noon we began taking down sails. By supper all were down but the foresail. Just after eating it was all hands again to take down the foresail. The wind had ripped it to rags. That night and the next day we traveled without any sails at all. Took all kinds of seas. The quarters had water on the floors, both lifeboats were full of water and one of them was smashed against the house hard enough to break the gunnel.

July 3

McPhee—Calmed down a little but have mountainous seas and heavy wind. Spent the day cleaning up wreckage. Couldn't do much with the deckload which is in a pretty bad way. Did the best we could with the lifeboats. Were going to raise the main or the mizzen but the lines were so fouled between the deckload and the rail we couldn't clear them so we raised the staysail jib. Worked only 16 hours today. Captain broke down today and said we could have anything we wanted to eat out of the storeroom. He is quite worried about the deckload because he gets 3 percent of it as part of his wages.

Bitte—Got up steam today but the seas were high and the weather too uncertain to hoist the main sails. Only raised the inner jib to give the ship steerage. Went to bed tonight after being up two days and a night, except for a couple of hours I got to lie down between watches and my own work to do.

July 4

McPhee—Oddest 4th I have ever spent, 600 miles from Cape Horn in the dead of winter. The moon was out bright at 7:30 this morning and the day broke cold and clear with a calm sea and moderate wind. All hands on deck, cleared the lines so we could raise the main, mizzen and spanker. The extent of fireworks was two fights between the bos'n and the Greek, one at 9 and the other at 11:30. There was such a heavy list to the ship because of the shifted deckload that they just rolled around not hurting each other to any extent. Everybody was getting irritable because of the general conditions aboard here and if they start taking it out on each other things will get worse. Another man laid up—the cook is in bed. Thinks he has a rupture or appendicitis. The rest think he is seasick. Things look bad for him if it is appendicitis. The sun at high noon looked like it was about as high as Council Crest. Logging about 5.

Bitte—Today was a holiday but was turned out at 5:40 this morning to raise steam. They put up three sails today and we were doing all right 'til now, but the wind is stiffening and we may have to lower sails before morning. The cook is sick with stomach, either a rupture or appendix.

July 5

McPhee—Clear and cold with no wind, doing about a mile at most. Would like to make some speed here and get around the Horn and up north where it is warmer and the days are longer. Dark from 4 to 8. They manage to work us Sundays, holidays, and part of our watch below aboard this tub. There was a tear in the staysail jib. We had to lower it and patch it this afternoon. The other watch claimed they didn't notice it until just after noon and it was too late for them to patch it. They are getting a big laugh out of it for their health.

Bitte—Sunday, and worked all day. Punched tubes and fired the boiler today. This makes 9 weeks at sea and I hope I never have to see another 9 on this workhouse. They have only half enough men on this ship and expect the carpenter to take up all the slack.

July 6

McPhee—Good weather with fair winds but cannot raise more sails because of the list caused by our shifted deckload. Put a splice in the inner jib stay and hoisted her back up. All the other jibs have shipping board splices which are three clamps. They give and slip so we will have to put regular splices in them or take chances of losing them during a blow. It developed that the cook has a bad rupture just to the right of his navel. It comes out quite a ways when he stands up and tends to make him sick. It was caused by the roll of the ship

101

Severe list of **Tango** *during a South Pacific storm. Donkey engine stack laid down. Photo by Ira Cheney III. (From McPhee collection.)*

Deck view of **Tango** *at sea, taken by Ire Cheney III from bowsprit. (From McPhee collection.)*

during the storm the other night, dislodging one of the stove lids which slid off the stove and hit him in the stomach. Some trouble over the cooking today, which had some humorous aspects. The Jew went to the Captain and was kicking about the grub. So the Captain ordered him into the galley to cook. Quite a scene was carried out before the Jew got out of it. He hasn't much to say since.

Bitte—Nice day today. Light winds and I wasn't hoping for more weather like that blow the other day. Slow but sure is my policy. The cook is apparently ruptured. As long as he stays off his feet he should be all right. The deckload shifted during the storm and we are having quite a time sailing on this tack. We should be rounding the Horn most any day and heading into warmer weather. It is about like November at home.

July 7

McPhee—Nice day with sunshine and fair winds, logging about 3 and still 370 miles from the Horn at noon. Saw a few flakes of ice which caused the Captain to tell us to be extremely watchful on the lookout.

Bitte—We are just about below the Horn now. If this weather will hold for a couple of more days so we can run to the east of it we will start north to a warmer climate. Remind me to tell you of the Jew being appointed cook by the Captain. It was the funniest thing that has happened to date. After all the arguments and fights it really was something. Sparks has been ahead some at rummy but I got one up today.

July 8

McPhee—Clear moderate weather with the Captain worrying because the glass is too high. An acute shortage of drinking water was revealed when the tanks were sounded today. Now allowed only a quart per man per day for drinking purposes and 4 quarts per day for cooking purposes. There is talk of stopping at the Falkland Islands for water. Spent the day restowing the deckload.

Bitte—Nice day today. The sun was up most of the day even though it doesn't rise much above the horizon in this part of the world. It was clouding up before dark tonight. May have some rain before morning. Are still sailing east so we must not be past the Horn yet. With the deckload shifted she doesn't sail very well on this tack.

July 9

McPhee—A blow hit us this morning. At 7:30 it was all hands and we lowered the main and mizzen. At 9:00, all hands and we lowered the jigger. The only sail we have up now is the staysail jib. The jibs are about a third as large as the other sails. Had a following sea so rigged up a barrel of storm oil aft. First time I have seen it used aboard a ship and it really does the trick.

Bitte—Forgot all about my Honey being a year older on the 7th of July 'til today. Hope she had a nice birthday. All the sails came down today but we are traveling right along. If the weather is improved by morning we will probably start north some time tomorrow and your Old Man will have rounded the Horn in a sailing ship. Some fun bouncing around and working like a dog—not quite.

July 10

McPhee—Double occasion today. First, it is my birthday and, second, we passed the Horn and were in the Atlantic about noon. Raised the main, mizzen and jigger and inner jib this morning but the ship listed so heavily because of the shifted deckload that we had to lower the jigger and inner jib. There are very few people who have celebrated their birthday on the exact day of rounding the Horn. We are now heading ENE. Will pass to the south of the Falkland Islands and then take a more northerly course. Nice clear, cold day with enough wind to do 5 knots.

Bitte—We rounded the Horn today. Cape Town can be made in 30 sailing days from here if we are lucky which we probably won't be. So the common guess is 45 days, or around the first of September, which is a long ways off. We hoisted sails again today and are moving along but not rapidly because of the bad list from the shifted deckload. May get a blow from the other side some day.

Chapter 8

Cape Horn

Old sailors called it "the Horn."

Across the Atlantic near the southern tip of Africa was "the Cape."

On the map Horn Island looks like the small end of a horn. But that was not how it got its name. It was named Hoorn Island after the home port in Holland of Willem Schouten, the Dutch sea captain who discovered the "Horn" in 1616 when seeking a new route around South America to the South Pacific spice islands.

Cape Horn is the southern face of Horn Island, a barren pile of rock five miles long lying in a northwest-southeast position. For three centuries it was an avenue of traffic between the Atlantic and Pacific Oceans, and it was notorious for its universally bad weather.

Located at 55°59′ South latitude and 67°12′ West longitude, it rises steeply to a height of 1,391 feet, the southern point of a mass of islands named Tierra del Fuego by Ferdinand Magellan when in 1520 he navigated the strait which later was named for him. The name is Spanish for "land of fire," the term he used to describe the lands along the strait because he noted many large fires built on the shores by near-naked stone-age type natives.

Cape Horn is 150 miles south of Cape Froward on the north side of the strait and the southernmost point of the South American mainland. It lies 1,300 miles south of the latitude of Cape of Good Hope, South Africa, and 600 miles south of the latitude of Stewart Island, the tip of New Zealand. It is a part of Chile, as is most of the Tierra del Fuego archipelago.

The "Horn" became notorious when sailors most feared its never-ending stormy weather. Prevailing winds blew strongly from the west, building up huge waves and strong easterly currents which propelled huge icebergs and ice flocs broken off from the Antarctic ice cap. Numerous ships disappeared without a trace in that area, Drake Passage, and were believed to have collided with icebergs or with groups of small islands. One massive berg was reported in 1893 to be three miles long and rising 1,500 feet above the water.

Some of the ship disasters occurred on the basaltic rock piles of the Diego Ramirez Islands, 56 miles southwest of Cape Horn. It has no lighthouse. Doors and other floatable debris from unidentified vessels have been found on beaches of the islands in the Cape Horn vicinity.

Ninety-six years before Capt. Schouten sighted Cape Horn, Magellan, a Portuguese navigator, was commissioned by King Charles of Spain to head a Spanish flotilla of five small vessels to search for a shorter route to the spice islands in the southwest Pacific than the long passage around Africa and across the Indian Ocean. He worked southward along the east coast of South America until on October 21, 1520, he came upon a passage that turned west. He named the turning point "Cape of the Eleven Thousand Virgins" (now Cape Virgins).

During the next month, he worked on through that broad waterway, generally to the southwest, then to the northwest, for a distance of 330 miles, coming out into the Pacific Ocean. The strait he had discovered was named after him.

One of Magellan's ships was burned in the strait, another ship and crew deserted, a third was wrecked, and the fourth was sent on an exploratory side trip to the western coast of South America and completely disappeared. Magellan continued with one small vessel to the Philippines, where he was killed in a battle between rival tribal chiefs.

Next to make history in this new sea route was Sir Francis Drake, an English explorer, who sailed November 15, 1577, from England with five ships to explore the coast of Patagonia and the Strait of Magellan enroute to the Far East. Arriving at the Cape of the Virgins, August 21, 1578, he made a quick voyage through the strait, arriving at the western end in 16 days.

In the Pacific he encountered strong headwinds which drove his ship, the *Pelican* (later renamed *Golden Hind*) southward about 300 miles. There he discovered a low island and anchored for four days. He called it "Elizabeth," after one of his ships. Long after he departed other explorers failed to find it and presumed it had been washed away by strong currents. More than 300 years later, in 1885, Capt. W. D. Burnham with the American bark *Pactolus* noted discolored water at Latitude 56°36' South, 74°70' West. Soundings found a water depth of 67 fathoms and a bottom of black sand and small rocks. It was then concluded that Elizabeth Island and Burnham Bank were the same and Drake's position was in error.

Drake eventually returned to England, the first master mariner to encircle the world.

Spain sent several expeditions to the strait to defend it against all others in an effort to control the new route to the southwest Pacific. But fatal illnesses contracted by crews and soldiers, and losses in fighting the savages who occupied the land took a heavy toll and defeated the Spanish effort.

Meanwhile, a Dutch expedition was financed by a wealthy merchant, Issac LeMaire, to seek a better route to the Far East. Under the command of Willem Schouten, two small ships sailed in 1615 from Hoorn, Holland. By-passing the Strait of Magellan, Schouten continued south to a passage he named the Strait of LeMaire and passed through, turning westward abeam the broken coastline until he came upon the small island which he named Hoorn Island. The date was January 29, 1616. This proved to be the southern-most extremity of the continent and the turning point of a new route to the Far East.

Eight years later a fleet of 11 ships was sent by the Dutch government to Cape Horn to chart and name the islands and channels behind Horn Island.

During the next century expeditions were dispatched to the area by Spain, France, Holland and England to cement their various claims of territory. Sea battles, founderings, sinkings, disease, starvation and deaths at the hands of natives were common.

Capt. James Cook made three voyages under the auspices of the British government to scientifically study the new lands. Twice he rounded Cape Horn during this period, 1769-1779.

In March, 1788, William Bligh doubled Cape Horn with his ship, the *Bounty*, but storms and currents carried him back eastward. On April 22 he gave up trying to regain his position and turned *Bounty*'s bow toward the Cape of Good Hope. A year later, Captain Bligh's crew mutinied in the South Pacific and cast him adrift with 18 loyal men. In their small boat the men sailed westward 3,600 miles before they found land. Bligh later served as an unpopular governor of New South Wales, Australia, in 1806.

Also in 1788, two small American ships, the *Columbia* and *Lady Washington* rounded the Horn, bound from Boston to the Northwest Pacific Coast to trade for sea otter skins. Four years later, Capt. Robert Gray, in the *Columbia*, entered the river he named after his ship. The discovery formed the basis of the U.S. claim to the Pacific Northwest.

The Fuegian archipelago was extensively surveyed and charted by a British party headed by Robert Fitzroy in two expeditions, the first, 1826-1830, the second, 1831-1836, using HMS *Beagle*. The first expedition surveyed the southern coast of Tierra del Fuego from the west end of the Strait of Magellan to Horn Island. Natives stole Fitzroy's best whale boat and it was not recovered despite a long search.

When he returned to England from the first voyage, Fitzroy took three native boys and a girl from Fuegian tribes, intending to educate them in England before returning them to their tribes as missionaries. One of the boys died in Plymouth and the others attended school for nine months before Fitzroy was ordered back to Tierra del Fuego to continue his charting. This cut short the education of the Fuegians. Fitzroy returned them to their families where they soon reverted to savage ways, disappointing their benefactor.

Fitzroy continued his surveys and charting while a companion, Charles Darwin, the young English naturalist in the party, studied and catalogued plants, animals and birds.

Fitzroy and six of his men landed on Horn Island April 20, 1830, with surveying instruments and climbed the mountain at the south end. They had a distant view in all directions and reported they sighted the Diego Ramirez Islands, 56 miles away, until haze blocked out the islands. While there, the men built a stone pyramid eight feet tall to mark their visit and toasted the King of England. some charts now show the peak as "Mt. Fitzroy."

During the 1800s the Fuegians were dying off rapidly, ravaged by white men's diseases and victims of firearms and fire water. Epidemics of measles and smallpox cut down whole tribes. One tribe in the Cape Horn area, the Yahgan, declined from 3,000 members in 1834 to less than 50 by 1924. By 1880 the country was sparsely populated, mainly by English, Scandinavians, Germans, Portuguese, and half-breed Fuegians. Very few pureblood natives were left.

The California gold rush, 1850-1860, drew a large number of sailing vessels carrying gold-seekers around the Horn. Some of these ships failed to show up in San Francisco.

During his memorable voyage sailing alone around the world, 1895-1898, Capt. Joshua Slocum had a confrontation with Fuegian Indians near Cape Froward in the strait. Anchored overnight, March 8, 1896, he took the precaution of spreading carpet tacks on the deck of the *Spray* before he laid down to sleep. He made certain many of the tacks were standing "business end up."

He wrote about it in his book, *Sailing Alone Around the World*, New York, 1900 (reprinted in 1956 by Dover Publications, Inc., New York).

"Now it is well known," he wrote, "that one cannot step on a tack without saying something about it. A pretty good Christian will whistle when he steps on the commercial end of a carpet tack; a savage will howl and claw the air, and that is what happened that night about 12 o'clock while I was asleep, when the savages thought they had me, sloop and all, but changed their minds when they stepped on deck for they thought that I or somebody else had them. I had no need for a dog, they howled like a pack of hounds. I had hardly use for a gun. They jumped pell-mell into their canoes, some into the sea, to cool off I suppose, and there was a deal of free language as they went. I fired several guns when I came on deck to let the rascals know that I was home, and then I turned in again feeling sure I should not be disturbed by people who left in so great a hurry."

He was not bothered again.

During America's war with Spain in 1898, the new battleship *Oregon* dashed through the Strait of Magellan under forced draft enroute from San Francisco to Cuba, where it helped win a crucial battle at sea. In 1907 sixteen ships of the U.S. Battle Fleet passed through the Strait of Magellan on their historic cruise around the world.

During the later days of the 1800s and the early 1900s, a fleet of European sailing vessels, mainly German, rotated around the Horn delivering coal and coke to South American copper mines and smelters, returning to Europe with nitrates, lumber and grain. At the same time steamships on regular schedules paraded through the strait, some around the Horn.

Then came World War I in 1914 which put a damper on Cape Horn passages when a pair of heavily-armed German cruisers, the *Scharnhorst* and *Gneisenau*, with smaller escorts, worked in the area to intercept enemy merchant vessels. They did some damage until a pair of British battle cruisers, the *Invincible* and *Inflexible*, surprised them near the Falkland Islands, sinking the *Scharnhorst* and prompting the German crew to open sea cocks and sink their *Gneisenau*.

The same year marked the opening of the newly-built Panama Canal which greatly shortened distances between the Atlantic and Pacific Oceans, virtually eliminating the Cape Horn-Strait of Magellan route.

During the 1930s a fleet of sailing ships, largely Finnish, participated in the celebrated annual grain races from Australia to Europe via the Cape Horn route. Among American shipmasters who made voyages around the Horn during the 1930s was Capt. Felix Riesenberg who made a study of the history of the area and wrote about it in his intriguing book, *Cape Horn* (Dodd, Mead and Company, New York, 1940). Among his conclusions he pointed out that although commercial shipping on that route had slowed appreciably, the Strait of Magellan has an interesting cruising potential for pleasure craft. The Tierra del Fuego is dotted with supremely beautiful towering snow-capped peaks, huge white glaciers, and enchanting channels winding between large and small islands, he noted.

The savages are gone, civilization is present. Population is growing. The principal city, Punta Arenas, a center of sheep raising, is a modern metropolis of more than 30,000, mostly European and Chilean.

The late Amos Burg, explorer, writer, photographer, explored the channels between Punta Arenas (which he called Magallanes) and Cape Horn for *National Geographic* Magazine and told about it in a 40-page, 40-photo article, "Inside Cape Horn," December 1937. With a companion, Roy Pepper, Burg made the adventure in a 26-foot ex-Coast Guard surfboat to which he had added a small cabin, an outboard motor, a mast and sail at his home, Portland, Oregon. The boat was launched at "Magallanes" and the men spent more than three months sailing and motoring through poorly charted channels winding among islands generally southward toward Wollaston Island, which lies next to Horn Island.

They visited the world's southernmost sheep ranch, an Argentine penal colony, and called upon natives, fishermen and hunters they found living along the way. The people were friendly and warmly welcomed the visitors.

But, Burg noted that the area lived up to its reputation of savage, uncomfortable weather. He mentioned a period of dismal, steady rain for 30 days.

Nearing the Horn the men came upon the world's southernmost seal and otter hunter, Ken Williams, who occupied a cabin about 30 miles north of Horn Island. Williams accompanied them to Wollaston Island where he and Burg climbed Mt. Hyde, 2,211 feet high, and viewed Horn Island about 16 miles away. They had a grand panoramic view of surrounding islands, Cape Horn and Drake Passage fading away toward Antarctica, 600 miles in the distance. The ocean was too wild to venture a visit to the cape itself.

Then, in 1974, Walker & Company, New York, published a book, *Children of Cape Horn*, by Rosie Swale, describing a 60,000-mile sailing voyage by her family—husband, Colin, children, Eve, 2, and James Mario, six months, when they left Gibraltar, December 19, 1971, in their 30-foot catamaran, *Anneliese*. They crossed the Atlantic to Panama, sailed on to Sydney, Australia, and Wellington, New Zealand, thence back across the South Pacific to Cape Horn, and home to Plymouth, England, arriving there July 1, 1973.

They passed Cape Horn February 8, 1973, summer in the southern hemisphere. Good fortune smiled on them in Drake Passage which they crossed without serious storms or extremely rough water, although the author admitted waves were "enormous." They saw Hermite and Wollaston Islands, shining glaciers and high mountains. The peak on Horn Island was visible for 40 miles. They were the first to sail around the Horn in a catamaran.

A Portland, Oregon, retired newspaper executive, J. Richard Nokes, saw the Horn from a Greek motorship, the *Illiria*, in January 1988, when gathering information for a book about Capt. Robert Gray, discoverer of the Columbia River. He flew from Portland to Santiago, Chile, via Miami, thence to Punta Arenas where he boarded the *Illiria*. The vessel sailed first to the Falkland Islands, south to the Antarctic Peninsula, back north to Cape Horn. Nokes photographed a beautiful rainbow arched beside the island. The Illiria returned to Punta Arenas via the Beagle Channel and Strait of Magellan. This was almost exactly 200 years after Robert Gray rounded the Horn with the ships *Columbia* and *Lady Washington*. Nokes' trip was arranged by Lindblad Cruises.

Cruises passing Cape Horn are offered occasionally by modern steamship companies. One such cruise was sponsored in January 1990, by the Smithsonian National Associate Program, Washington, D.C. 20560. This was summer in the southern hemisphere when weather is usually fair.

The Smithsonian tour began at Miami, Florida, January 17, where the party boarded a Chilean Air Liner and flew to Santiago, the capitol of Chile, for two days of sightseeing. The group was then flown 500 miles south to Puerto Montt, a city of 52,000 at the north end of the inside passage between the mainland and a system of islands lying off the southern west coast of Chile.

At Puerto Montt, the party boarded a smart new luxury cruise ship, the *Seabourn Spirit*, of 10,000 tons and flying the Norwegian flag, for a two-day voyage down the inside passage. It paid a one-day visit to Puerto Natales, then continued around the southern coast of Tierra del Fuego to the Horn, then north to the Beagle Channel and the port of Ushuaia, the Argentine capitol of Tierra del Fuego, and southernmost seat of government in the world.

The *Seabourn Spirit* cruised west and north through exciting channels to Punta Arenas, for a brief call, thence east in the Strait of Magellan to the Atlantic Ocean. It went north

Cape Horn from south. Photo by Fred Van Raden on cruise liner **Royal Viking Sky**, *Feb. 14, 1990. Mrs. Corrine Van Raden smiles happily.*

to Montevideo and Buenos Aires. Passengers were flown 650 miles north to the spectacular Iguassu Falls before boarding a plane February 3 to return to Miami.

Shortly thereafter the *Royal Viking Sky* made a similar voyage in the opposite direction with 600 passengers. It departed from Rio de Janeiro February 5, called at Buenos Aires, Montevideo and Puerto Madryn before arriving off Cape Horn in the evening of February 14, Valentine's Day.

The ship hove-to for about four hours while a small motorboat carried several passengers to the island where they visited a modest dwelling for the keepers of a lighthouse maintained by the Chilean government on the tip of the island. The vessel circled the island before turning north to Beagle Channel, thence to Punta Arenas for a day's visit. It cruised west through the Strait of Magellan, thence through the Chilean fjord country to Puerto Montt and Valparaiso, arriving February 21.

Mr. and Mrs. Fred Van Raden, of Portland, Oregon, who were among the passengers, reported this was an exciting and beautiful experience. Weather was pleasant but chilly.

The 17 men on the *Tango* who dared to sail through the tempestuous Drake Passage in mid-winter 1942 were favored by relatively mild weather, according to the brief reports by Archie McPhee and Fred Bitte. But they did not see the Horn. It was either too far away or was hidden behind clouds, mist and rain. They accepted the Captain's word for it.

Chapter 9

The Horn to the Cape

July 11

McPhee—No entry.

Bitte—You know this life is monotonous—just one hardship after another. We have a nice breeze and good seas now, but can't carry enough sail to take advantage of it on account of the shifted deckload. If it isn't one thing it's another.

July 12

McPhee—Nice warm day with sunshine but only a 2-knot wind. Good news today: We are going into Montevideo, Uruguay. The deckload is shifted so bad it has started to bend the rail and if the rail gives way it might tear off the top plate or tear a hole in the deck where the stanchions are. The only bilge pumps we have are run by electricity from the diesel engine and the wires to it have become severed beneath the deck and they have to be fixed. We also have to do a lot of work on the rigging. The distance from our noon position to Montevideo was about 1,200 miles, which we ought to do in two weeks. While they were feeding us salted ham, the good canned hams spoiled—24 of them—real economy.

Bitte—Sunday again, and 70 days at sea. Nice weather with a gentle breeze. Salt water got in my light conduit and now I have to bring a wire over deck for lights. There is some talk that we will sit in Montevideo to straighten out the deckload and pick up drinking water, but it isn't likely.

July 13

McPhee—The Captain has been reconsidering his decision to go to Montevideo and will make up his mind definitely in the next 4 or 5 days. He is afraid of raiders north of 40 deg. and unless something develops might not call in. If we go in there it will be termed an emergency port and they won't have to give us a draw. By the crew not having any money left there will be a strategy on the Captain's part not to give us a draw. The only one on board with any money is the Jew, who has about $20 in cash and $250 in traveler's checks. Everyone on board is trying to get in good with him so they will be able to borrow money off him. It is a funny situation. Only a couple of days ago they were ribbing and teasing him, but now he is a great guy. He is not as dumb as they think he is, though. He told me last night the only ones he would loan money to were the bos'n and myself. Clear cold weather with no wind.

Bitte—Got the wires laid on deck and have the lights on aft. We hoisted another sail today. It will have to come down at the first sign of a blow. The rumor still persists that we may go into port to fix the ship and get her on even keel again. Before we start across the Atlantic will know for sure in about four days.

July 14

McPhee—Cloudy and cold with a headwind against which we are making no headway but are being blown sideways. Things are going from bad to worse. Doing some work on the lifeboats and found they are both rusted out at the keels and are absolutely unseaworthy. Cook is having internal hemorrhages. Nobody seems to know whether it is a bad sign in case of a rupture. Rowley, O.S., gets over his bum ankle but doesn't seem to like this bum weather so he is now feigning appendicitis. He complains of a sore side, then goes to bed, puts on an act like he is out of his head, but doesn't groan or act up when nobody is around. They have come up to his quarters several times and caught him reading. He then drops the magazine and goes into his act. His temperature is normal and so is his appetite. The Greek has been cooking the last couple of days and he has the rest of them beat a mile.

For example, he made some spaghetti which became a shake of being as good as what Hilts and I made.

Bitte—We have more reason than ever to go into port now as both lifeboats have holes rusted through them and we are raising quite a sea now. Are encountering headwinds so we aren't moving much. Hope tomorrow is a quiet day so I can't get at one of the lifeboats and plug the holes with solder, which is the best use we have for it on this ship to work with—no acetylene outfit.

July 15

McPhee—Cold and clear with a headwind that keeps us at a standstill. Rowley is still keeping up the appendicitis act. The sailors' term is "Cape Horn Fever." A whale of the blueback species and fully 90 feet long nosed around the ship for half an hour today. He was as large as any of us aboard have seen. The cook told me today he thought he was going to die. The Captain doesn't seem to think it is serious to vomit blood, though. And the Captain is the law aboard a ship.

Bitte—Stiff wind tonight and we are traveling right along. Put patches on one of the lifeboats today with metal screws. Lucky I brought mine along. Will solder around the patch tomorrow if the weather allows. Doubt if it will be calm enough, though, the way it is blowing up. Got myself almost caught in a swell that broke over the deck. Today pretty cold to get wet now.

July 16

McPhee—Same weather as yesterday. The bos'n went to Rowley and told him to cut out the acting as people don't get delirious unless they have a fever, and that his temperature is normal. If he didn't go to work at once, the bos'n would see that he didn't get back in the sailors' union. It proved to be the best medicine in the world. Rowley was back on deck at noon just as healthy as ever. If you look at him or grin, he gets red from the collar to the hairline. Instead of calling into a

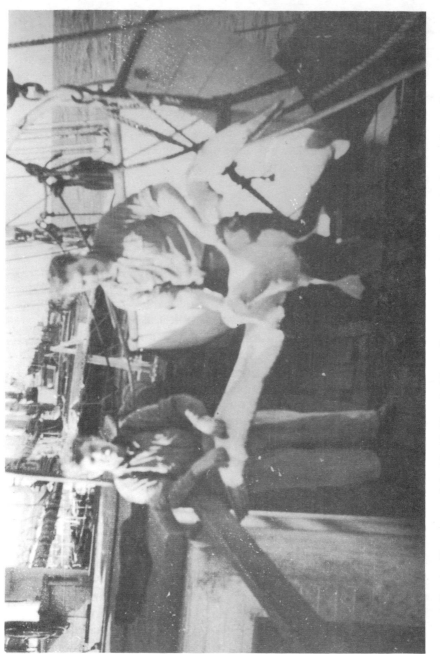

Charles Hammer and Archie McPhee hold an albatross, in South Atlantic. (From McPhee collection.)

port, the Captain is figuring on letting the deckload go if we hit any more rough weather.

Bitte—Still headed northeast. We are somewhere above the Falkland Islands but I don't know just where. The sun hasn't been out for several days so the Captain is just going by dead reckoning and we seldom hear where we are unless he gets a shot at the sun. Didn't do a very good job of soldering around the patches on the lifeboat. May have to do something else on them before I am through.

July 17

McPhee—Clear and cold with the wind and sea picking up. Wind has shifted and we are doing about 8 knots. We have gone farther in the last 10 hours than we had in the previous four days. Started to bend in a new foresail this a.m. but wind and seas picked up so much we had to stop. We have eaten better in the last three days with the Greek cooking than at any other time during the trip, but he is going to quit in the morning—alas and alack. The messboy got mad and threw a deck of our cards in the slop bucket this a.m. So we threw his deck overboard, put red pepper in his tobacco can and finely cut-up rope yarns in his bunk. The Captain said if the fellow didn't straighten up he was going to lock him up and stop his pay. Lots of penny ante stuff going on.

Bitte—Nice clear day and we got our position. We have hardly moved in the last four days. We are at 54 deg. 9 min. below the Equator and intend to run up to 40 deg. before cutting across to Africa. Tony, the Greek, is cooking good. That is excellent compared to what the other fellows are doing.

July 18

McPhee—All hands on deck at 4 a.m. to take in the jigger. At 11 a.m. the wind had torn a two-foot rent along the leech and pulled out five hanks on the inner jib so we had to take it in, too. Snowed twice today. Sea tore up the deckload and shifted it some more. Picked up some giant albatross. Looked like they had about 15 feet wingspread. Talked the Greek into staying in the galley for a while longer. He is the only one who can make the salt pork and beef taste good.

Bitte—Rough today but not a gale. Got some pictures of big waves today. Took the last of the Kodachrome roll and put the Super X into the camera. Have been thinking quite a bit of home lately and you and the boys doing all right. Bet the garden is doing well. Wish I could be there to help keep down the weeds.

July 19

McPhee—"Red Sails in the Sunset." Prettiest sunset I have ever seen. Set about 4:30 with just enough clouds that were not too heavy to obscure but lent a pattern of various colors. Where there were no clouds the sky was deep red. And, strangest of all, the sky above was dark blue enough that the moon and a few stars stood out fairly bright. During this time the white sails looked quite red. Coldest weather we have had yet. Making about two knots.

Bitte—Nice today, but windy this evening. Moving along about 4 knots. Wish we could get farther north and out of this cold, but the wind is driving down at us from the north. So most of our course is to the east and not much at that as we are trying to head the ship into the wind in an effort to get farther north. At 52 deg. below today.

July 20

McPhee—Repaired inner jib, set it, the outer jib and the jigger. The reason the inner jib was damaged in the blow the other day was because it wasn't set right. The Captain isn't going to let the other watch set any more sails because they have shown themselves to be incompetent and the mate is too lazy to care. Unusually cold but we have a fair wind now and are making 5 knots. Talked the Greek into going back into the galley. He uses a lot of garlic and onions in his cooking and I like it.

Bitte—Almost calm this morning. The boys raised another big sail and also the outer jib. The wind is quite stiff this evening but the seas are calm and we are traveling right along. Wish we could have this weather all the time. Was this our wedding anniversary?

July 21

McPhee—Wind changed to southwesterly and brought us a nice snow storm. Jibed over with ice and snow on deck, which caused the jigger tackle to get away from Hammer. When the boom swung over it knocked four of us flat, seriously injuring Ira Cheney, O.S. on our watch. He got two bad gashes in the head and either a bruised hip or broken one. With the wind on our other side, the ship isn't on an even keel because of the shifted deckload. Making about 8 knots.

Bitte—We made good time last night and today I finished soldering the lifeboat and fixed the inside with cement. Hope we don't have to use it as I don't feel she is too seaworthy. Probably better than no boat at all. The sailors are jibing the ship over right now. If the wind will stay on the starboard side we would make some good time. Hope the family is well and making out all right.

July 22

McPhee—Snowed all day. Heavy wind, had to take in the outer jib. Ship's list should be to the lee side, but because of our shifted deckload our list is to the weather side. Because of this we ship a lot more seas than ordinarily. The seas are pounding the deckload over a bit and might straighten her out. The seas and wind keep most of the snow off the deck. Doing about 8 knots, with 2,300 miles to go at noon yesterday.

Bitte—Made good time today but a little too rough to suit me. The elements don't go out of their way to please me. Certainly will be glad to see the last of this boat ride. Have been thinking about the asparagus. Hope it did well. What I wouldn't give to have a mess of it and fresh peas, topped off with strawberries and cream. Boy, I can torture myself by thinking about it out here. Snowed today.

July 23

McPhee—The mate was steering six points off the course this a.m., ESE instead of ENE. The wind had shifted and he should have jibed over but instead he goes off course and leaves the jibing over for us to do. This kind of stuff leaves hard feelings between the watches. Rain, snow, sleet and hail all day. Storm got bad—had to lower the jigger, mizzen and inner jib. Only the staysail jib and main up now. Putting out storm oil. Doing about 6 knots. Had a snatch block dropped from the pin rail of foremast rigging. It fell about 15 feet and hit me on the right knee cap. My leg is pretty sore and badly swollen.

Bitte—Rough weather today, and the talk is we have about 2,000 miles yet to go. Should make that in 20 days if we have any luck at all. It is a clear night with scattered clouds so we should have a fairly clear day tomorrow even if the wind doesn't let up. Hope they got a shot at the sun so we know where we are. Made a plunger for the electric water pump that I use to supply water to the diesel engine out of the sole of one of Archie's old shoes.

July 24

McPhee—As we came on watch at 12 this morning, the wind worked the mousing on the sister hooks of the staysail tack loose and the sail was flying in all directions. Quite a job to secure it. Repaired it on our watch on deck this a.m. Set it and the mizzen. Nice night with the moon shining and the sea and wind calmed down. Had a real disappointment today. The Captain found he had made an error of 400 miles in figuring the distance to go. It wouldn't have been so bad if it had been 400 miles less, but no such luck.

Bitte—What a day. The machinery is going to pieces faster than I can fix it. Hope things are right in Cape Town so

I can get a freighter for home. Tired tonight, am going to hit the hay early.

July 25

McPhee—Warmer with a fair wind, logging about 6. Put up the outer and inner jibs today. Steers a lot better. Our latitude is 45 deg. S. We are out of the iceberg infested zone but are in raider infested waters and are observing the strictest of blackouts. The Greek had me write an argument for him to have the Captain sign. It was to the effect that he would get steward's pay while he was cooking and also that the Captain would pay him off at the first S.A. port. Both the Greek and Moeller have had their citizenship papers taken away and we were told they could not land in the U.S. again. Both are branded as labor agitators. The Greek was telling us that at his last trial, which was after Russia entered the war, they dropped a charge of communistic activities brought against him previously.

Bitte—Got the plant running again and the weather is quite a bit warmer so things look rosier. Did my white laundry this afternoon. Will do my shirts tomorrow and probably some pants. I hope that will be the last I have to do before reaching port. I'll let a laundry do them there. The news coming over the radio isn't so good with Russia about to lose the Caucasus and Rommel in Egypt.

July 26

McPhee—Noticeably warmer, still have a fair go at about 6 knots. Cheney is feeling quite a bit better. He is going to have a bad scar on his forehead. Set the jigger at 11 a.m., then the barometer dropped at 4 p.m. Had to lower it and the outer jib. Saw a couple of whales. They seem to be quite a bit larger here than those off our west coast.

Bitte—Gosh, I was thinking today it was only a couple of years ago that we were married and started to figure, then realized it is over 7 years already. Gosh, how time does fly. Wish it would go that fast this next year, but it won't away from home like this. 'Tis heck for a fellow who likes to know how his family is making out. Sure worry plenty about them. Hope the boys didn't get hurt in the cherry tree this summer.

July 27

McPhee—Three months wages coming today—85 days at sea without sight of land or another ship. Wind shifted to due south so we jibed over to a starboard tack. Had the company of 300 strange birds for about 6 hours and then they flew off elsewhere. They were identical to swallows in build and flight but were as large as common seagulls, with white bodies underneath, gray on top and black fringe around the wings on top and underneath. Bright moon tonight, almost as bright as day.

Bitte—Payday again. Hope things have gone well and the mortgage is paid off, but mostly you and the boys are well. Enjoy the summer. It has been rather cool here as the wind shifted to the south during the night. The ship has been on an even keel all day. It's swell not to have to walk at an angle all the time. We are halfway across the Atlantic now and may make it in three weeks if we have any luck at all.

July 28

McPhee—Becalmed since 1 a.m. Nice warm day, it is early spring down here. Comparable to March in Portland. No wind, so it was all hands and we finished bending on the foresail. We raised the foresail and the jigger. Most of the sails we have had up for more than a month. Inner jib, staysail, foresail, main, mizzen and jigger. About 4 p.m. a wind sprang up from the SE so we had to jibe over. Well rewarded for a hard day's work we had macaroni and cheese for supper a la Greek. Had as pretty a sunrise as I have ever seen. The moon is full tonight and everything is bright as day. Cheney got out of bed today.

Bitte—Nice spring day, makes one think of garden and home. I do hope that at this time next year I am enjoying my home and family instead of thinking and longing for them.

I'll never leave this long a time on my own free will again. I didn't know that the minutes would be as long as they are here. They always went so fast at home, and it isn't because I haven't got enough to do. I have plenty.

July 29

McPhee—Inner jib stay, which is 1½-inch wire, got loose about 11:30 last night. It was quite a job securing the sail as a strong wind sprang up. Spliced and put up a new stay on our deck watch this afternoon. Days are getting longer which makes for fewer lookouts to stand. The diesel motor generator gives off static which detectors can pick up so they have quit using it. It is almost warm enough that we have quit using the kerosene heaters. The sea is calm enough we can keep our door open. This all tends to do away with fumes which have bothered me and I feel like a new man. We are doing a lot better with the foresail up. It eliminates a lot of pitching, which makes the ship easier to steer and we can make a knot or two more an hour. Distance to go is 1,600 miles and we are logging about 7 knots. If we keep this up we will make it in 10 days. The Greek put out a dish tonight that he calls shrimp jambolai. It is steamed rice with a shrimp sauce over it and it was really good.

Bitte—Didn't do much today except punch tubes on the boiler and take a bath out of a bucket. Boy, am I looking forward to a bath in a tub in a couple of weeks if we have fair winds and a little luck. The little plant failed me tonight and I ran the big one for lights. Played cards with Sparks. While I was watching the plant Sparks got five games ahead.

July 30

McPhee—Some heavy weather today with rain squalls. Had to lower the jigger and jibe over. Damned lucky nobody was hurt when we jibed. Had two boom tackles on the mizzen and were slacking on them when a big gust of wind filled the sail, broke both of the tackles and the sail slammed over miles an hour. Reeling off 7 or 8 knots. Finally cleared up tonight.

Bos'n got mad at Sparks, the radio operator, and slapped him around a bit. Kind of bad, the kid is only 19. Spaghetti and meat balls for supper—really good.

Bitte—Stiff wind today. They say we are less than 1,500 miles from Cape Town now. If we can hold yesterday's speed we can make it in 10 days, but that isn't likely to happen. I'll bet Steven is getting to be quite a little rascal by now, but he should be getting a better break than Larry did as Larry should help keep him out of trouble. My guess is that Larry is just about ruling the roost with you.

July 31

McPhee—The wind being from the south we are having another taste of winter weather. It was cold today and we had snow. Picked up some giant albatross today. The bos'n was going to try to hook one and caught two of them in his triangle at one time. The double weight broke his line and they got away. Making 7 knots.

Bitte—Ninety days at sea and all we have seen so far are sea birds and a few fish. May sight an island this Sunday from what I hear on the grapevine. It is 1,200 miles from Cape Town so someone's figures yesterday must have been wrong. Really don't care if we sight the island as long as we get into port soon and I can find out how the folks at home are making out, and if they are well and in good health.

August 1

McPhee—Sheet on the staysail jib carried away this a.m. We repaired it and set it again on our watch this a.m. Two stars were coming over the horizon early this morning. Cheney spotted them and excitedly turned them in to the mate as an airplane. Still making about 7 knots. Nice day with the sun shining.

Bitte—Well, another month started. They all seem alike out here. We should make port in about two weeks if we have any luck. It's about time we have a little and make port without any trouble. The bos'n and Sparks have had a little trouble. Most of the fellows are on edge and a little touchy. Have been out too long a stretch.

August 2

McPhee—1,180 miles to go at noon and now our speed has gone; lucky if we have averaged one knot since this a.m. Passed between Gough and Nightingale Islands today. We were within 55 miles of the latter and as it is 1,100 feet high we could have seen it had the day been clear. This island is the mating and nesting ground of penguins. 'Tis said they are so numerous on this island during the mating season you cannot walk anywhere without stepping on one. Spent the afternoon, which was nice and warm, setting the jigger and fishing for albatross. I am getting pretty bad. Was trying to catch one myself and incidentally came closest to getting one. Had him right up to the counter when the ship sat down and the wash knocked him loose from the triangle. There are only three of them following the ship but they are monsters with about 15-foot wingspread.

Bitte—We had a very nice day today but the wind is shifting tonight and the barometer is quite high so we may have a blow. Hope not. Passed that island that is 1,200 miles from Cape Town but didn't sight it as far as I know. Today was Sunday and I took it easy. Tony, the cook, fixed up some swell eats today, and the prospect of reaching port in a couple of weeks is enlightening. That Sparks is running me a close race for the malteds. I may buy them yet.

August 3

McPhee—One hell of a miserable day and evening. Ran into a bad blow and it was all hands at 6 a.m. to lower the jigger and foresail. Shipped some awfully heavy seas which knocked our deckload back into place. The Captain was running around like a madman all day, watching the steering and checking the compass. We are supposed to be within 30 miles of an island and the wind is too strong to jibe over without lowering the sails, and jibing then setting them again.

Cannot do that because the diesel engine is on the blink. We are having to steer a point over course. This, along with slippage sideways, we are getting close to this island. Lowered the mizzen tonight at 10. Have up only the main and staysail. Doing about 6 knots.

Bitte—Strong winds are carrying us south of our course. If the diesel hadn't broken down we would have dropped the sails and jibed over, but it was just past midnight before we got up steam so they decided to wait until daylight to do it.

August 4

McPhee—A heavy rain beat the wind and sea down. We are now becalmed. Set the jigger, mizzen and foresails this a.m. Rerove the hanks on the inner jib and set it. This is my dear brother John's birthday. Methinks he may be celebrating it in some army camp. Another mistake in navigation. It was supposed to have been 1,180 miles to go Sunday. The Captain worked his charts over and found it to be 1,220 miles today. After all his worrying about running ashore last night, he found we were more than 100 miles off it.

Bitte—The wind shifted before daylight came so they upped the sails this morning in a calm. They say we are about 1,100 miles from Cape Town. At the speed we have been traveling that is only about 11 days sailing. Hope we have a little luck and make it in that time. If we do, I won't have to wash very much clothing before we get there. Not much of a laundryman.

August 5

McPhee—Becalmed until 4 this p.m. Wind came up from the NE. We jibed over and set the outer jib. Making about 2 knots. The clock in the messroom could be seen only from one side of the table so I moved it. Jones, who is on the other watch, claims he was the runner-up champion in the Golden Gloves lightweight division for 1932 and thinks he is pretty tough, didn't like my moving it and behind my back referred to me as that "one-eyed guy." I waited for him to come off

130

the wheel this a.m. and called him on it. He didn't prove to be so tough and apologized.

Bitte—Nice sailing weather today but time is dragging now that we can see the end of the voyage in sight. Some of the more optimistic men still feel we can make it in by the 14th of this month. Worked on the diesel today. Made some straps to hold the base plate on. It has a crack down the center of it. Finally got ahead of Sparks at rummy. If my luck will hold out a few more weeks, I may drink malts on him yet.

August 6

McPhee—The wind shifted to NW and is fair for us now, and we are making 7-8 knots. Rowley and the Greek had a fight over a crib game today. The Greek got the best of it. We are now in the most dangerous waters of the trip. The convoys to the Red Sea and Egypt pass through here. Consequently these are hunting grounds for German raiders and submarines. Absolutely no lights. Northerly winds are supposed to be the warm winds here, but the one we have now has icy fingers.

Bitte—Boy, this is too good to be true. Two good sailing days in a row and we are making good time. The sea has just begun to get a little rough but if it doesn't get worse we probably will get through the night without lowering sails. Well, it is about the latter part of summer at home and the boys are spending quite a bit of time at the tank. Hope you are well enough to be there if you wish to.

August 7

McPhee—First thing we came on deck this morning we had to jibe over. The other watch, instead of jibing, left the work for us and steered six points off the course to keep from doing it. The wind is now from the SW and plenty cold. 840 miles to go at noon, barring mistakes in navigation. Getting things ready for port. Put up the fish tackle which is used to take the anchor off the deck and hang it over the side. Overhauled the anchor windlass. Got the mooring lines out of the forepeak. All these preparations make one feel good after being out 100 days. I went about two-thirds of the way up the jigger via the hoops to cut a hoop adrift after it had broken down. Making 4 knots.

Bitte—Sailing along nicely but most of us are impatient to get into port. No more electric lights until we are in port as we are approaching the shipping lanes and they are afraid of subs picking up the disturbance from the generator. The word is that we have 840 miles to go but the rumors have been wrong often. We have been at sea too long for me.

August 8

McPhee—Becalmed at midnight. Not enough wind to keep the sails full but enough puffs to keep them slapping back and forth. This slapping broke the boom tackle and boom lift of the foresail and put a two-foot tear in it. All hands at 1:30 to take the foresail down and secure it. When we came on at 4 o'clock there was a little wind and when we took over the wheel the other watch was steering west. They were 14 points off the course just to hand the work of jibing over to our watch. The bos'n read the first mate the riot act. The other watch repaired the foresail and we set it in the p.m. I did a dastardly deed this afternoon. I caught an albatross and killed it just to get the feet and beak as souvenirs. The Captain got one also. They were both beautiful birds and it was a dirty shame to kill them. Mine had a 13½-foot wingspread and the Captain's had 12 feet. Nicest day we have had since rounding the Horn. Making about 2 knots.

Bitte—The foresail broke loose during the night and the boys had it lowered when I got up this morning so they repaired it and we got it up again today. No wind during the day but it is blowing now. The Captain and the bos'n caught themselves each an albatross. I got pictures of the bird the Captain caught on deck and some feathers to bring home to the boys.

August 9

McPhee—Plugging along about 4 knots and only 650 miles to go. Had a meeting today and made a long list of demands to give to the Captain, but it doesn't make him happy, either. Captain and mate cleaned one of the albatross and ate some of it for supper. None of the crew would eat any. Nice, warm sunny day. Not a bad ship on a day like this. It is also the first Sunday in two months we haven't had to work.

Bitte—The ornery little Sparks is here talking while I write this, saying we can count the remaining days on our fingers. But 14 weeks at sea can't be counted on your fingers. It's too darn long. The work is easier now that we are having better weather, but I can't make port too soon to suit me.

August 10

McPhee—Ran into a good blow at noon and the wind changed. Too much wind to jibe over and had to sail west until 4 o'clock before we could jibe. Went about 35 miles back toward Portland. Now headed in the right direction and making as much as 10 knots. Albatross steaks for dinner and supper. The only ones to eat them were the Captain, mate and the Greek. The Jew was on the warpath today and tried his damnedest to pick a fight with somebody on the other watch but nobody would take him on. Skinned my albatross feet and beak today. After having gotten hurt twice when jibing over, Cheney is afraid of it and has an awful time getting himself to go out on deck when we are doing it.

Bitte—Are less than 500 miles from Cape Town and traveling fast. Hope to spend the weekend in port. It will be nice to sit down to a decent table to eat. And just about my fondest dream is to be able to soak in a hot tub of water for a couple of days. Am playing rummy desperately with Sparks. He is three games ahead at this writing and his luck is still with him.

August 11

McPhee—Lost our wind and were becalmed this morning, but 'twas not so with our Captain. The Jew, who is our delegate, went to the Captain with the list of demands from our meeting on the 9th. The Captain flew into a rage and we could hear him hollering all over the ship. He threatened to handcuff the Jew to the rail and to have the whole crew jailed on arrival. The Jew, being very aggressive and union-minded, never gave an inch of ground and he was in the saloon arguing with the Captain an hour and 20 minutes. Funniest incident: The Jew told the Captain that upon arrival he was supposed to get ice for the icebox and then fill it with fresh fruit, vegetables, milk, etc. The Captain replied, "Instead of getting ice for the icebox, I am going to get straw and put in three live pigs for you." The Captain hasn't sailed since our 1934 strike and doesn't want to recognize the conditions we gained at that time. Had an albatross aboard, took some pictures of it and let it go. Wind picked up at six and by midnight we were doing about 8 knots.

Bitte—Took things easy today. Even turned watchmaker and worked on saloon clock. Don't know whether I did it much good. Got it to run but haven't been able to slow it down. Took some pictures of a whale and birds today.

August 12

McPhee—325 miles to go at noon. Have been making 6 and 7 knots all day. Radio operator picked up an SOS from a ship that was being attacked off the South American coast by a surface raider. Everyone is shaving his beard, polishing shoes, etc. Nice weather so I took a bath and discarded my long-handled underwear. Had an escort of six whales most of the day. Two of them were babies and the others 80 to 90-foot monsters.

Bitte—Too close to port to do much work. Less than 285 miles to go. Should make it with good luck in 48 hours and I'll be able to find out how the folks at home are making out. Got over the radio last night that an Axis raider was operating in the Southwest Atlantic. We got out of there just in time if that is so.

August 13

McPhee—180 miles to go at noon and we have lost our wind. Killed an albatross accidentally. We were catching them and bringing them aboard, taking pictures and letting them go. The fourth one put up an awful struggle and swallowed so much water he drowned. We gave it artificial respiration but to no avail. Shook the reefs out of the jigger, mizzen and main and took an inventory of the stores. To make it look like there were a lot of stores, they filled the storeroom actually half full of flour, beans and rice. There are better than 200 sacks of flour, 25 sacks of beans, 25 sacks of rice, ten cases of toilet paper, enough spices and condiments to last 10 years, 200 cases of pilot bread which is only flour and water crackers, 750 pounds of coffee, and enough breakfast foods to last a couple of years. Other foods, practically nothing. I got pretty sick working in the storeroom. There is no ventilation and a lot of dust from the flour, and musty odors. Lucky if we made 20 miles from noon to midnight.

Bitte—Less than 200 miles to go and we have been becalmed. It is starting to tell on the tempers of the crew—just too long at sea in one stretch. Wouldn't mind being in port myself. Right now this ship is like camping out—one has about the same facilities for keeping clean.

August 14

McPhee—130 miles to go at noon. By 6 p.m. we had such a strong wind the Captain ordered the jigger and outer jib down. He is afraid we might get too close to land before daybreak. I climbed up the forward mast at 4 p.m. to see if I could see land but no luck. The Captain is going to take the lock off the water tank in the a.m. so we can have some water to wash clothes. Happy day. Three months and 12 days without seeing land or another ship.

Bitte—Less than 100 miles to go and lots of wind. They lowered some of the sails tonight so we wouldn't get there before daybreak. They are afraid of running into a mine field during the night. Hope we put into Cape Town and aren't ordered on to Durban. Hope, hope.

August 15

McPhee—This was the day. I went up the mainmast at 8 o'clock and about 8:15 I saw a ship approaching from our starboard quarter. It was quite a while before they could see it from the deck. The thoughts were: is it a raider, a patrol boat or a submarine? It turned out to be a freighter headed for Cape Town, also. Couldn't see land by 10 o'clock so I came down. Went up again at 12:30 and lo! and behold! there was Table Mt. I was the first to sight another craft or land after 105 days at sea. At noon we had 58 miles to go. Got within 20 miles at dark so we had to turn back to sea. Had quite an escort of sea gulls come out to meet us. They look awfully small alongside the albatross. Schools of seals playing and fishing around the ship all day and until we went off watch at midnight. It was a bright moonlight and it was interesting to watch the seals fish. The phosphorus waters outlined every move of the seals and fish. The seals made a noise just like laughter. Maybe they were laughing at us. Shaved my whiskers today. Jibed over three times tonight and lowered the staysail jib.

Bitte—Land ho! We sighted land today but head wind prevented us from reaching it. Also sighted some ships, the first signs of life since we left the river. It does the spirits good to see signs of life after 105 days. Don't know where we will be in the morning the way the wind is blowing now.

August 16

McPhee—Headed for sea until 6 a.m. and damned near didn't make it back by dark. Radio operator is a 18-year-old kid who was going to school when he got this job; signed on for $345 per month. His first bit of work was messages by blinker light from shore. He couldn't get it and we didn't have room enough to turn around so the Captain kept her straight ahead. It was kind of dangerous because they might have been sending a warning of mines or something. Finally got a pilot and tug who took us to an anchorage in the outer harbor. First things the Limey did was to bum us for American cigarettes. Complete blackout of ships lying at anchor and there are quite a few of them. Lot of lights ashore and they look pretty good. Pilot told us the *Star of Scotland*, same rig as this ship, took 127 days to our 105. She lost her deckload and they had to go 30 miles out to sea to tow her in. Also the company was going bankrupt and the crew was having a hell of a time getting any money. It is the same old company we are working for—worry, worry. Had a nice workout today. On deck from 4 a.m. until midnight working and now I am on anchor watch from midnight to 8 a.m.

Bitte—At anchor in the outer harbor at Cape Town. We dropped anchor about 8 tonight. Boy, it is swell to see city lights again. Won't get ashore here unless we dock and discharge.

August 17

McPhee—Saw the sunrise this a.m. Cape Town is very pretty. It is built at the foot of Table Mt., which rears up abruptly behind. There is an inner harbor and an outer harbor. We are in the outer harbor waiting for orders. There were no orders waiting for us so we are waiting for an answer to a cable we sent to New York. Couldn't go ashore so we spent the day washing, fishing, sightseeing. Lots of marine life in the harbor but all we could catch was sand sharks. There is a school of seals playing around and fishing around the anchored ships. There are also eider ducks, who are by far the best fishers amongst the birds we can see. Doctor was aboard. Cook has to go to the hospital for his bad rupture; messboy has to go to the hospital also—venereal disease. Carlson to the hospital with pleurisy. McPhee, water on the knee and cracked kneecap, ashore for x-ray and treatment.

Bitte—At anchor in the outer harbor. We have been cleared by the immigration. Now we are waiting for the Captain to make up his mind that we can go ashore. He has been there all day. It is heck to be this close to town and not to be able to get to it and wire home. Would also like to get a haircut and bath. We got fresh milk and vegetables today, and also some fruit. It was great after being without them.

August 18
Bitte—Got ashore tonight and sent a wire home. Cost just about $4.00 for two words. Boy, are prices high here. Also went to a show and slept at the Seamen's Club after the show. That is one thing that is reasonable, a bed and bath for about 35 cents, American money. Can't say I like it here.

(Note—Two words in wire: "Arrived safely.")

August 22
Bitte—Had to look at the calendar to see what day it was. Went ashore on the 19th to see a doctor about a pain in my chest and they ran me all over town till it got so bad I had to put up at a hotel overnight to get over the cold chills that set in from muscular rheumatism in my chest. Damned painful, like a knife being poked through my chest. Wrote home airmail while in town but don't remember what I said.

(Note—Later, Bitte wrote that the ship remained in Cape Town for one week to straighten out the deckload. But it actually stayed there more than two months. The shore gang failed to tighten chains and the load shifted again enroute to Durban. The company finally sent pocket money to the crew, but most allotments were sent home.

Bitte tipped a boy $1.00 to carry a heavy bag to the Seaman's Club. Police came to the club and got after him for giving the big tip—too much. Should have been a "tickey," worth three cents, U.S.)

P.S.—Bitte bought the milkshakes in Cape Town and Sparks enjoyed his fill.

Chapter 10

The Unhappy Crew

The long voyage from the Columbia River to South Africa was not a bed of roses for the 17 men on the *Tango*. From the very start at St. Helens, Oregon, the men worried about their futures and their families in the event they were attacked by an enemy war vessel because they had discovered the 38-year-old metal lifeboats were badly rusted and pitted, with small holes in the bottoms. Going to sea in one of them would be like riding in a sieve.

The boats' condition was called to the attention of the captain and others in authority but no action was taken to repair or replace the boats. The ship sailed from St. Helens and later from Astoria with the lifeboats lashed to davits which the crew members claimed were out of order and should have been repaired before the vessel sailed, according to statements by crew members after the ship reached Cape Town.

Two of the men declared they worked for several hours to repair an electric bilge pump that could not be primed while the ship was at sea. Complaints were made that errors apparently had been made in the rigging.

Inadequate and poorly prepared food was another source of annoyance throughout the voyage and the captain and cook were besieged with demands for improvement, generally without result until the cook was hospitalized and others took to the galley. Then, Angelo Varellas, the Greek A.B., won plaudits for his imaginative spicing up otherwise tasteless fare.

The general attitude of the men was one of worry and despair. Some of them wished they were not aboard. They were not allowed to go ashore during the four days the vessel was anchored off Astoria so there would be no last minute escape. On the way down the Pacific Coast at least two men wanted to be let off at Long Beach, but the captain laid a course well out to sea. There was no further chance for a man to get ashore.

The ten deck hands organized crew meetings to express their dissatisfaction by drawing up petitions and demands to the captain for some measure of relief. The motivating force in this behavior was Ablebodied Seaman Joseph Kaplan, "The Jew" in Archie McPhee's log. Joe and Archie were cabin-mates and members of the same watch. They became fast friends and in later years when Joe came ashore from time to time in Portland between steamship runs he left personal papers with Archie for safe-keeping. He had no permanent home. After Joe died of cancer, McPhee still had Joe's file and it contributed to this chapter about the unhappy crew.

Joe Kaplan, a lifelong professional seaman, was a feisty little guy, a staunch union man with strong communist leanings, and stood on his principles. He was somewhat of a sea lawyer with the welfare of his shipmates at heart. He dominated crew meetings and became the crew's delegate for confrontations with the anti-union captain and first mate after others failed.

Joe was not afraid of Captain Gundersen or anyone else and refused to be turned back when the captain threatened to have him put in irons and jailed for insubordination. In fact, he threatened the captain with charges of violations of the union contract and failure to consider the safety and welfare of his men. He threatened to have the captain jailed in Cape Town.

When the ship finally arrived safely in Cape Town, Joe led crew representatives in visits to the U.S. Consul to com-

*Deck crew of **Tango** in first meeting to select a delegate to represent the crew in negotiations with the Captain. (Barber)*

Ablebodied Seaman Angelo Varellas at work bench. (Barber)

plain about conditions on the ship and to charge the captain and owners with various federal violations.

There is no doubt that Joe Kaplan contributed to the unhappiness of the crew, but he stayed with the ship to the very end of its American ownership after most of the other men had been paid-off in Cape Town and Durban to return home. He was the most colorful and respected man aboard.

To get a crew, the Transatlantic Navigation Company, Inc. signed contracts with the Sailors Union of the Pacific and the Marine Cooks and Stewards Association of the Pacific Coast. The marine cooks agreement was signed April 13, 1942, by Asa F. Davison, vice president of TNCo., and Roy Lawyer, representing the union. The SUP contract was signed April 25, 1942, by Davison and J. W. Massey, the SUP agent in Portland.

The SUP contract provided that the Second Mate-Bos'n would be paid $425 a month; the donkeyman-carpenter, $325; the ablebodied seamen, $310; ordinary seamen, $257.50. The cooks and steward's contract provided for payment of $412.50 a month to the cook and $292.50 to the utility-messman. These were the highest wages paid to a crew on any of the ships that sailed from the West Coast to South Africa during that early war period.

Working rules provided that customary ship's work, such as painting and chipping, be done between 8 a.m. and noon, and 1 p.m. and 4 p.m. No overtime pay would be given for work performed at sea, but overtime work in port would be paid at the rate of $1.35 per hour after an eight hour day. Saturday, Sunday and holiday work was to be paid at the overtime scale.

"It is further understood that the Master shall see that this agreement is lived up to at all times, the only exception being the safety of the vessel, its passengers, cargo and crew," the agreement stated.

Each man was to be furnished clean white linen once a week, consisting of two sheets, one pillow case, one bath towel, two face towels. In the absence of clean linen, the crew was compelled to wash its own and to be paid one hour overtime. Soap, matches and blankets were to be furnished by the ship.

In the event the vessel was wrecked, sunk or sold or the crew interned, the crew was entitled to wages until returned to the original port via first class transportation. In the event crew members's clothing was lost due to shipwreck or sinking, the men were each entitled to $300 for the loss of clothes.

The company agreed to cover each crew member with an insurance policy of $5,000 for loss of life due to any hazard of war. Before clearing a U.S. port, the company agreed to place $25,000 in escrow account with the Bank of California, Los Angeles, Cal., to guarantee crew members their wages for the southbound voyage.

The agreement with the marine cooks' association was similar. It provided for meals at 7:30 to 8:30 a.m., 12 noon to 1 p.m., and 5 to 6 p.m. It also required that officers' quarters to be made up daily by the utility-messman, listing the captain, first and second officers, and radio operator.

In the crew meetings, there were complaints that some of the provisions were not adhered to, and when the ship arrived in Cape Town there was no agent to meet the vessel and no funds awaiting to pay-off crew members or cover other expenses of ship or crew.

In fact, after the men returned home some of them declared they felt the owners had no intention of paying because they did not expect the ship to survive.

"They had it greatly over-insured," said Fred Bitte, the carpenter. "We were told that in Cape Town."

* * * *

J. Ferrell Colton, in a letter dated May 26, 1987, said:

Mr. Fred Bitte is *quite correct* about the matter of over- insurance. You can quote me, also, on this subject. As acting Master of the schooner, I took her out of the sectional floating drydock on the morning of 10 September 1941, and moved her, with two tugs, some 2.5 miles up-harbor. That is, from the drydock's location on the north side of Smith Island to the Turning Basin at the confluence of the main channel, West Basin, Slip No. 1, and East Basin Channel. San Pedro Lumber Company's wharf was about two-thirds of the way up the East Basin Channel. After my crew of a dozen drunken union runners left, I made a complete inspection, as is my custom in such circumstances, of the entire sub-waterline areas of the vessel's inner skin. All was in order until I overlooked the forepeak. There, somewhere below the 8' draft mark and well below the existing waterline on the starboard side, I discovered a stream of seawater, under pressure, coming inboard through a pencil diameter hole in a bow plate. I immediately reported this to my superiors, Captain Davison and Mr. Pernikoff, the alleged owner. In essence, I was told to mind my own business and not to mention the matter to anyone. At this point in time, all the parsimonious planning and construction that I had observed (and objected to) added to a total I realized that it was the owner's hope that the schooner would never reach her destination . . . That is the main reason I turned down the offer of the Second Mate's berth. Bitte had every right to be bitter . . .

In another letter December 9, 1987, Colton added that Captain Davison remarked to him in effect: "She is heavily insured." Colton also stated, "my temporary wooden plug was still in place shortly before she sailed for the Columbia. She was not drydocked again prior to sailing for Africa."

*　*　*　*

The captain went ashore the first day and cabled New York for funds and instructions, but crew members were not allowed to leave the ship for several days except three men who were sent ashore by a doctor for hospitalization.

But the biggest gripe among the crew was the deplorable condition of the lifeboats. Several men signed individual statements. James E. Burke, the second mate, and Joe Kaplan signed a joint statement addressed to the captain charging that holes were in the bottoms of the boats before the ship sailed from St. Helens and the captain's attention had been called to the matter, but no repairs had been made.

Angelo Varellas addressed a long undated letter in which he declared he noted the condition of the boats when he was employed by Albina Engine & Machine Works as a rigger on the *Tango*. He said the davits and falls were in dilapidated condition. After he signed on the Tango April 28, he said, there was no fire or lifeboat drill as required by law. He said he and the carpenter worked for three hours at sea to prime the bilge pump, but without success. During a storm at sea, the port lifeboat was smashed against the house and damaged and leaking. He pointed this condition out to the chief officer but no action was taken.

Following arrival in Cape Town, nine members of the crew filed a complaint with the U.S. Consul, August 20, charging the vessel was unseaworthy and requested a survey of the lifeboats and pumping equipment. It was signed by James E. Burke, second mate and bos'n; Joseph Kaplan, Charles Hammer, Archie McPhee, Hans K. Moller, Howard Jones, George St. Clair, ablebodied seamen; Ira Cheney III, ordinary seaman; and Eugene Luce, wireless operator.

On September 1, Kaplan and Jones visited the consul and pressed for a survey by three men to be appointed by him, instead of one representative of the American Bureau of Shipping as the consul had proposed. The consul informed Kaplan and Jones that if the inspectors found the ship seaworthy, the crew would have to pay the cost of the survey, and if the survey found the ship unseaworthy the company would pay. If the ship was found unseaworthy, the crew could sign-off with an extra month's pay and transportation home.

The consul said the company would send enough money to cover immediate needs and to pay-off two sick men, but not $30,000 due the remainder of the crew. It wanted the ship sent on to Durban to discharge its cargo.

"We told the consul the owners wanted to get us to Durban so they would be in the clear in regards to their contract and there give us a screwing, and the consul agreed that might be the case and promised again that he would see that the maritime laws were lived up to in this port, and we would get everything we had coming according to law," Kaplan and Jones reported. Their statement was written on letterheads of the Merchant Seamen's Welcome Club, of Cape Town.

Kaplan and Ira Cheney later issued separate statements regarding the lifeboats addressed to the American Consul. Cheney added: "I can also certify that when Captain Gundersen attempted to rectify any unseaworthy condition with the owners or agents, he was informed that he could leave the vessel if he did not like the vessel's seaworthiness."

Four weeks after arrival at Cape Town, members of the crew drew up a long epistle addressed to their union leaders in San Francisco deploring the conditions under which American seamen went to sea on sailing ships hastily restored and sailed, similar to the *Tango*. The handwriting of the copy left with McPhee resembled that of Kaplan's and there is no doubt he had an important part in preparing it.

Dear Sir and Brothers:

The crew of the S.V. *Tango* wishes to inform the membership of the Sailors Union of the Pacific of a few interesting and important facts in regards to sailing ships hiring through our union halls and signing agreements with our union. The owners of these vessels have no intention of living up to their agreements with the union and are using the war

147

effort as a screen behind which to make enormous profits.

As proof of this you have only to check with the American Consul in the big South African ports and you will find that on no U.S. sailing ship since the war have the crews received their just wages. On a couple of vessels the crew are receiving African pounds a week so as to pacify them but although the *Tango* has been in port for three weeks, the crew hasn't received a sou. The Old Man sailed without a cent in the safe and wasn't even furnished with a letter of credit by the owners.

It seems these ships receive their freight money as soon as the vessel puts out to sea. The prepaid deal comes under the lend-lease system, so it seems, and having been paid already they don't give a damn whether the ship is unloaded or not.

The S.V. *Tango* hired a crew in Portland, Ore., on April 27th and 28th. The crew reported to the vessel on the 29th and she left at 12 noon for Astoria the same day and anchored out in the stream with none of the crew getting shore leave. After a few days in the stream we sailed for South Africa. It wasn't until we were under sail that we found that the reformed gambling ship was unseaworthy from stem to stern and that the "old man" and mate were a couple of Bowery "bums."

Not only did the overhead leak, but both lifeboats were full of holes, with no life raft aboard. The electric pump for the bilges was broken with no way of fixing the damned thing, and besides the ship is without a hand pump. The rigging bands on the masts have slipped down a foot. The ship has a fourteen degree list here at anchor. The skipper and the mate are a couple of "hoodlums." The holds are half full of water. We put in 105 days at sea and have been at anchor here four weeks and haven't got a draw yet.

When our delegate went to the Old Man with the overtime sheet, the old goat threatened to put him in irons, hit him on the head with a belaying pin and throw the key away. What sort of stuff is that? When bad weather came, the captain crawled into the nest and didn't get out until the blow was over. This happened a number of times. In warm weather he would come out and catch albatross, knocking them over the head as fast as he pulled them in, bringing much bad luck to everybody. It's a wonder nobody was killed.

This letter is being written with the intention of wising the membership and officials up to the get rich guys who buy an old hulk cheap, fit her out with sails and hire a crew of union men at double wages with no intention of paying the crew.

Food situation: We were informed when shipping that there were eight thousand dollars worth of stores aboard but after we got out to sea we learned from the steward that there was only about two thousand dollars worth aboard, and on inspecting the stores we found the salt horse to be rotten, the salt fish to be rotten, the canned goods to be the lowest kind and most of the cans were marked "below U.S. standard." Things are sure going to hell when union men have to put up with that kind of stuff.

Overtime: On six occasions when our ship's delegate, Joseph Kaplan, went to the Mate and the "old man" to check overtime they always put up hot arguments. The two old boys had never checked overtime before and threatened to put half the crew in irons for demanding overtime pay on a sailing vessel.

Protecting Seamen: The crew feels that they are entitled to some measure of protection from the union and would like to advise our officials to get on their toes and keep an eye on these phony sailing vessels and crooked owners.

Two watch system: Back in the big blow-off of '34 we abolished the two-watch system and here eight years later we have the two-watch sail-ships hiring men through our halls and like damn fools we find ourselves going aboard and manning these vessels. It's about time we got wise to ourselves. There's enough room on a sail ship for three watches as there is on a steamer.

That was the last of the long Kaplan-like letter to the Sailors Union of the Pacific headquarters.

It must be remembered that this letter expressed the foc'sle viewpoint of an excitable, tough union man and the more radical fellow members of his deck crew. Some of the men, and probably the majority, appeared to like the captain but they did little to interfere with Kaplan's abrasive attacks on the captain.

"I liked the captain and respected him greatly," said Gene Luce, the radio operator and only apparent survivor of the crew. "He was the old sailing ship type and was not used to the rigid demands of the unions. In fact, he had not sailed with union crews before he came to the *Tango*.

"In spite of the charges alleged in the letter, he never was drunk, although he liked a glass of wine. He never went to bed to lie out a storm, as the letter asserted—no way. Joe made those charges in anger. He and the captain ranted and raved at each other when the captain rejected the union demands.

150

"I know that Archie and Ira Cheney also liked him. Archie simply reported what happened when he mentioned the quarrels in his log."

The captain and mate were recruited in Brooklyn, not in the bowery of New York, despite the assertion in Kaplan's letter. In fact, Kaplan also was from Brooklyn, born there May 6, 1911, of Jewish parents. He died of cancer in Portland, Oregon, September 7, 1974, at age 63, a seaman for 42 years. After the *Tango* experience he was in steamships for about 30 years, frequently as a union delegate.

Efforts to locate the captain's official log were unsuccessful so his side of the story was not available. It would have been most interesting.

Chapter 11

Cape Town to Durban

The *Tango* remained in Cape Town two months and 22 days to restow the deckload, refit rigging and sails, and make other repairs. It provided a welcomed R and R for crew members who went ashore when the captain doled out a little draw money to them. They did what sailors do when they go ashore. They visited the bars, movies, dancehalls, the Seamen's Club, and girls. In fact, a couple of them paid for their adventures with VD. The Cape Town girls liked American sailors because they were good spenders.

Fred Bitte was on the verge of a nervous breakdown when the ship arrived and spent some time with doctors for treatment of a pain in his chest. He hoped to get a berth on a steamer for home but was unsuccessful and stayed with the *Tango* for the run to Durban, its destination.

Archie McPhee went sightseeing. He took a train to Johannesburg and Kimberly, a round trip of about 1,800 miles. And he went to the top of Table Mountain for a fine panoramic view of Cape Town and Table Bay.

One of the joys of the Cape Town sojourn was fresh milk, eggs and fruit, in contrast with the miserable grub the men endured during most of the voyage when the milk and fruit were gone and the eggs were fished out of brine. McPhee said they tasted flat but Bitte claimed they were good.

With repairs to sails and rigging completed and the deck load lashed down, *Tango* sailed November 6, 1942, for Durban, leaving behind the original cook, messman, two ABs, Angelo Varellas and George St. Clair, and Ordinary Seaman Mural "Swede" Rowley. They were replaced by five other

*Part of the **Tango** crew on deck (left to right) Jos. Brown, Joe Kaplan, Archie McPhee, Ollie Lindberg and John Maddison on deck. Indian Ocean. (From McPhee collection.)*

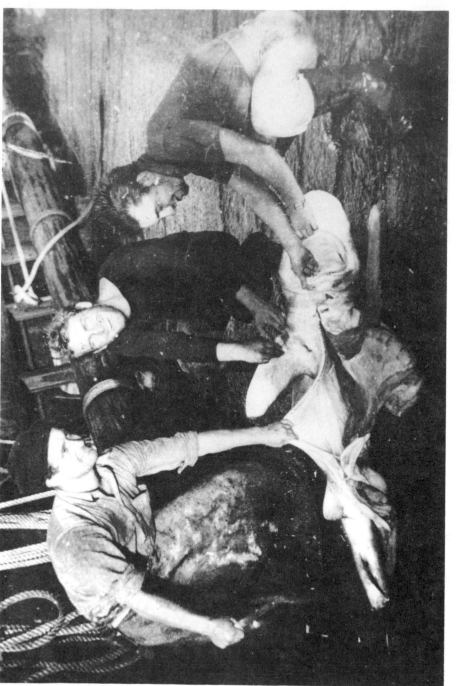

Harry Pearce, Ira Cheney III and Charles Morgan dissect a shark, Indian Ocean. (From McPhee collection.)

men, including an Australian and a Finn. A kitten also joined the crew.

The steamer distance to Durban is about 750 miles, but the route taken by the *Tango* was 2,000 miles. To stay away from the rocky coast of Cape Agulhas, the southern tip of Africa, the captain laid a course westerly from Table Bay for more than 200 miles to avoid adverse currents, thence south to the "Roaring Forties," and east several hundred miles in search of southeast winds to blow the ship northward to Durban. By keeping well away from the coast the ship avoided enemy submarines and raiders.

It proved to be a long and arduous voyage beset with adverse winds and currents, the vessel barely crawling along and actually drifting back at times. There were days when the wind blew exactly opposite to what the ship needed and other days when there was no wind, leaving the vessel a sitting duck in case an enemy war vessel appeared. One day the ship was carried 40 miles backward.

All the time the crew feared being attacked by an enemy war vessel and the men slept with their clothes on and their personal papers in their pockets, ready for quick abandonment of the ship. They passed through floating debris from other vessels, apparently sunk. One day the men on lookout spotted a pair of men's socks floating by and wondered who may have been the owner and what may have been his fate. One night they saw lifeboat flares rising in the sky several miles ahead, but they never caught up with another ship or lifeboat.

Bitte said later, "I got a kick out of old Charlie (Carlson) counting his beads. He was scared."

The *Tango* was sluggish from layers of barnacles on the bottom which reduced its speed by one-third and steering was made difficult. Work on board was hazardous because the lumber deckload now was two feet higher than originally piled in Oregon. The deckload soon shifted, causing a troublesome list.

Changeable winds kept the men busy lowering, then raising sails, and patching the rotting rags as fast as they blew out. They worked many hours overtime, sometimes two or three watch periods without a good rest.

For diversion, some of the men tried fishing off the poop or catching albatross alongside. Fishing for tuna was not productive, but a few big birds were brought aboard, fed salt pork, photographed and released.

The chief mate went to bed with a rupture and the new ordinary seaman broke out with VD. Three men had scabies and the radio operator broke his glasses. Another man developed appendicitis. That totaled seven ailing men out of 17 on board.

And the second mate and the messman had two fist fights. A big happy family?

By December 7, the first anniversary of the Japanese attack on Pearl Harbor, *Tango* had crept close to Durban but became becalmed in dangerous waters. To her relief came a tug which towed her into the harbor, where she remained for six and one-half months. The lumber cargo was discharged piece by piece by hand, and then the vessel was loaded with coal for Santos, Brazil. On the day she was to depart, a tug assigned to tow her out recklessly slammed into the *Tango*'s bow, cracking three plates. The ship returned to her berth, discharged part of the coal cargo and then went to a shipyard for renewal of the broken plates.

Again the sailors spent time ashore doing the things sailors do. McPhee, the good-looking boy from Oregon, was invited to dances. The new cook acted queerly at times, according to Bitte. It was learned later that he was indulging in alcoholic extracts—vanilla, banana, lemon—from the ship's stores and got a bit high. In fact, he fed some to natives working on the ship and they danced and sang until they got too much and couldn't stand.

When ready to sail again, several of the original crew members paid-off to return home and were replaced by sailors of other nationalities. The new crew included three South Africans, and one each Irish, English, Australian, Finnish and Norwegian—truly an international crew with the seven original Americans left, a total of seven nationalities.

Of the original crew, only Captain Gundersen, Chief Mate Peter Holt, Second Mate Hans Moller, Radio Operator Gene Luce, and ABs Archie McPhee, Joe Kaplan, and Ira Cheney were left. Cheney had been promoted to AB. Paid-off in Durban were Fred Bitte, the carpenter; Jimmy Burke, the original second mate-bos'n; and ABs Howard Jones, Charles Carlson, and Chuck Hammer, of the original Oregon crew.

Bitte caught a ride to New York on the British steamship *Athlone Castle*. His place was taken by Richard Berlin, of Seattle, who had survived the sinking of the *Star of Scotland*. Also a new member was "Tango," a wirehaired Scotch terrier. He made it eight nationalities on board.

Tango finally sailed June 12, 1943, for Santos. She was under the American flag, but an agreement had been reached by her owners for her sale to a Portuguese shipowner and delivery in Brazil. This voyage turned out to be more of the same—but worse. The first day was pleasant except that heavy swells caused the ship to roll wildly from side to side. The weight of coal in the lower hold caused the vessel to swing like a pendulum, according to McPhee.

Then, on the third day, a storm broke with tremendous seas pouring over the deck. Sails began to come apart—first the flying jib, then the spanker, followed by the foresail and the mainsail, each tearing into shreds. With the decks constantly awash, there was extreme danger of men being washed over the side, and one of them, Henry Pearce, the new English ordinary seaman, almost got it. Another man caught him in the nick of time. The crew's quarters were flooded and the men were soaking wet for 24 hours. The next two days were spent clearing up the mess.

157

During the first week the ship made good only 200 miles in the right direction, all the time it was in dangerous waters. Again, the men slept with their clothes on.

This condition continued for more than five weeks as *Tango* was buffeted by high winds and huge seas, tearing up nine of the 11 sails she carried. The men were kept busy mending canvas when not raising or lowering it, or dragging it in from over the side. On one occasion, two were wrestling with the steering wheel when a big sea came over the poop and knocked Henry Pearce through the wheel, breaking out one-third of the spokes, and throwing Ollie Lindbergh over the rail and into the rigging, which luckily kept him from going over the side. There was no possible way of rescuing a man lost overboard in that treacherous ocean.

The quarters, radio room, carpenter shop, carpenter's room, the hospital, cook and messman's quarters were all flooded. There was some grousing about cold food because the cook could not keep pots and pans on the stove. Joe Kaplan, as the crew's delegate, complained to the captain, who threatened to lock him up. Some of the salt beef spoiled and crew members tossed two barrels of it over the side.

After weeks of severe buffeting and torn sails, the captain abandoned hope of going to Santos and decided to try to make it into Cape Town as an emergency port. Unable to make headway toward Cape Town, the captain considered going back to Durban, or even to East London or Port Elizabeth. When he finally decided to beat back to Durban, he asked crew members to sign the log saying the vessel was unseaworthy, as a protection to him. The men were happy to sign.

On fair days the men amused themselves by catching albatross, which were plentiful. They danced with the big birds to music from an old phonograph which had been given to the ship in Durban. The birds were placed on deck between a house and bulwarks where they could not escape. The men danced to the music toward the birds which would back away, doing a sort of dance step. Then the men would dance backward and the birds would follow. Even the dog took part, getting too close to the birds and getting his nose nipped.

"It was really funny," said McPhee.

The ship worked slowly back toward Durban, bucking an opposing current which flowed southwesterly along the African coast. Finally, on July 20, a convoy passed and a destroyer came close enough to inquire where the *Tango* was headed, but raced away before Captain Gundersen could request a tug. *Tango*'s radio was out of commission. The destroyer captain apparently understood *Tango*'s predicament and passed word to shore because two small patrol boats came out and one towed the ship while the other circled about to give protection.

The ship and men returned to the same port they had left 38 days before. All hands agreed they had been through weather worse than any previously experienced. Only 15 days out of the 38 were decently comfortable, according to McPhee's log.

Now, let Archie McPhee and Fred Bitte fill in the details:

Chapter 12

The Cruel Sea
Archie McPhee Reports

Friday, November 6, 1942

McPhee—Sailing today for Durban. *Star of Scotland* sailed last week for Brazil. We were here two months and 22 days and it is with pleasure that we leave. My most lasting impressions of Cape Town are the panoramic view from the top of Table Mt. and the seals and penguins playing in Table Bay. Might be a waste of writing this because there is a lot of submarine action between here and Durban and I might never get it to the States.

Bitte—Under sail again. Have been under sail since 10 a.m. today, and are still in sight of land. The breeze is freshening up tonight but from the wrong direction. May have better luck tomorrow. It shouldn't take more than two weeks to reach Durban from Cape Town with luck. It's good to be on our way as it will be that much sooner we can start on the long trip home.

November 7

McPhee—On a starboard tack, heavy wind blowing us inshore. We had to lower the driver and the ship was so sluggish from barnacles it took us two hours to turn around and we were in danger of going aground. Had quite an escort of seals and have picked up some albatross and Cape Horn pigeons. Have five new members in the crew:

Cook, Jack Hancock	in place of C. LeMon
Messman, Willie Green	in place of W. Hahn

AB, R. A. Brown (Australian)   in place of A. Varellas
AB, John Sampson   in place of G. St. Clair
AB, Ollie Lindbergh (Finnish)   in place of S. Rowley

Really have a good cook this time, but the doctors have given him only two months to live because of a bad heart. Also have added a kitten to our crew.

Bitte—It looks like a long trip to Durban as we are having to go west to clear the cape. If we don't get more fair wind by morning, it probably will be a month at sea before we reach port. Never get home at this rate.

November 8
Bitte—Sunny, and still going northwest from Cape Town. Right on the route to New York.

November 9
Bitte—Not much wind today, but we are sailing SWxS, so we eventually get below the cape if the Atlantic is wide enough.

November 10
Bitte—Same as yesterday except not quite as much wind. Ho hum, what a life.

November 11
Bitte—14 deg. East and 35 deg. South today with a fair wind from the southwest so we are finally sailing in the right direction.

Thursday, November 12
McPhee—The difference from Cape Town to Durban is only 750 miles by steamship route, but we may have to go about 2,000 miles to get there. We have to go west about 200 miles to get away from currents, then south to the Roarin' 40s, then east and pick up a southeaster and ride it into Durban. Since Friday we have gone only 240 miles. Were becalmed Tuesday and Wednesday. Slushed down the jibboom with fish

oil and linseed Tuesday. Quite a bit dropped into the water and the albatross had quite a time playing in it. We have 18 of them hanging around and caught just about every one of them and had them aboard for a while. It is evidently mating season for the albatross as they are doing quite a bit of fighting and what appears to be love making. The males trumpet like drakes with their heads and wings straight up in the air. They have been interesting to watch and we would not have been able to see them had we not been becalmed. We jibed over today and now are heading south.

Bitte—Still traveling, only 4 sails up now, but it looks as the wind won't get any stiffer. May have to raise another sail tomorrow. Hope not.

November 13

McPhee—If they don't get us today we should make it all right. Everybody is sleeping with his clothes on and his papers in his pockets. We are now headed southeast by south. The ship is so sluggish from barnacles we had to lower the spanker so it would steer. The barnacles cut down our speed by a third.

Bitte—Calm today and the sun was out so we got our position. Even with all the wind we had moved only about 200 miles in 48 hours. The bottom of the ship is too cluttered with barnacles to make any time. Will be a long trip to Durban.

(This was Bitte's last entry.)

Sunday, November 15

McPhee—In a blow we worked all our day off. Had to take in the flying jib, mizzen, jigger, and spanker and then the wind broke the sheet on the outer jib and it took us better than an hour to get it in. They did such a poor job of restowing the deckload in Cape Town that it is now two feet higher than before and makes us top heavy. The load is now shifting to the starboard side. Doing only about 4 knots with a wind that we should be able to do 8 with.

Monday, November 16

Put in single reefs in the main, mizzen, and jigger; double reefs in the spanker and driver. Repaired outer jib, which had about a dozen rents in it. Our only motion is an easterly drift with the current.

November 17

Quite a few little incidents today. Ran through some large patches of oil slick this a.m. Either a steamer or a sub must have been sunk in this area. Had some yellowtails and they are pretty marked—bright yellow tail, brilliant green body, and light blue fins. We couldn't catch any, though. I finally figured a way to catch the little Cape Horn pigeons and with my bare hands I caught seven. We took them aboard, fed them, took their pictures and let them go. I hung over the side at one of the water ports which is just above the waterline. Had one of the fellows drop a little piece of pork into the water. The birds are pretty wary until they start to fight over the meat. Then we could catch them. On my first grab I caught two. I also got good and wet as the roll of the ship put me in the water. The chief mate is in bed with an old rupture which he has torn some more. Lindbergh, the new O.S., has broken out with a venereal disease. Sampson, Sparks, and the cook have scabies. Sparks has broken his glasses. All the fresh stores are gone. To top this off we are averaging about 35 miles a day with ideal weather conditions most of the time.

November 18

Becalmed. Nice warm weather. Had 27 albatross swimming around the ship. Great sport catching them. Also caught more Cape Horn pigeons by hand. Tied meat on each end of a string. Lot of fun to watch when an albatross gets on each end. We were lassoing them today. I'm getting good enough with a palm and needle that the bos'n lets me patch sails and today had me making a dodger.

November 19

At 4 this a.m. the ship decided it want to go NW and there wasn't a thing we could do about it until 5 p.m. At 8 tonight we saw lifeboat flares. Figured they were 5 to 8 miles ahead of us. If they have a sail up they are probably going faster than we are. The 2nd mate and messman had a fight today and as a result the messman has gone on strike. I don't blame him, either. I caught a couple of albatross by hand today. The Captain wanted to keep them and have fresh meat for Thanksgiving, but we said we wouldn't eat them and let them go. Had quite a workout this a.m. trying to turn the ship around. Jibed over four times and slacked the sheets out several times and pulled them back in. At the rate we are going now we will be lucky to get there by Xmas. This should have been about a 10-day trip.

November 20

This ship has some sort of curse on it. The messman has infection in his jaw from a blow in the fight he had with the bos'n. Brown's appendix is bothering him and he throws up green matter. That's six or seven men with ailments now. We could not find a trace of the lifeboat which fired the flares. The ship is so unmanageable that we couldn't tack back and forth to search for it. Captain approached me today and asked me to catch 20 Cape Horn pigeons so we could have a meal, but I refused.

November 21

Heading due east with a fair strong wind. Making an average of 4½ knots for last 24 hours. Made a ditty bag and packed it with a few necessities for the lifeboat. They were: 1. My heavy woolen shirt. 2. Horlicks lunch tablets. 3. Matches and cigarettes (not for myself). 4. Jar of Vick's vaporub. 5. Can of pineapple juice. 6. Some pictures of the trip which I would hate to lose. 7. Army sewing kit and palm, needle, and sail twine. 8. Heavy wool socks. 9. Writing material for notes, and deck of playing cards. 10. Sunburn lotion.

We are not allowed to take anything bulky or unnecessary into the boats, but I had all this packed in a small canvas ditty bag and I think I will be able to get away with it.

Sunday, November 22

Little wind but we have a 2½-knot current pushing us along. Couple of us were standing on the foc'sle head and saw a pair of socks float by. Wondered as to the story behind them. Some big whales played around us for a while today.

Friday, November 27

Big school of whales playing around ship this a.m. Cook came out of his quarters still quite sleepy, saw some of them coming toward the ship. He thought it was a torpedo, began to run and holler. In dangerous waters 450 miles from Durban at noon. Second mate and messman had another beef today. I got to put a patch on inner jib this afternoon. Saw a big school of tuna yesterday, but nobody could catch any. Have been on this ship seven months today. Held a meeting and drew up a list of demands. Don't expect to get any of them, but nothing like trying.

November 28

Headwinds and also a current against us. This is one spot where we could use favorable winds. Passed through the wreckage of a ship—some hatch boards and wooden bulk-heads. Had to take in outer jib because of tear along the leech. Staysail halyard busted and she dropped. With the wheel hard over the ship wouldn't steer, so we had to lower the main.

November 29

Wind changed from NE to SE, now fair for us. Set the main, repaired and set the staysail, and jibed over twice between 4 and 8 a.m. Wind picked up this afternoon and we ran into an electrical storm. At noon Saturday our position was 36 deg. 40 min. south and Sunday it was 37 deg. 4 min. south. Because of headwinds and currents we had lost 40 miles.

December 2

Ran into a blow at 3:30 p.m. All hands on deck. Lowered spanker, jigger, flying jib, inner jib, outer jib and staysail. Leech started to tear on main so had to lower it. Shipped big seas but they were warm; we didn't mind getting wet. Made more miles from 3:30 to midnight than we have made in the last three days.

December 3

Heavy seas and wind but making good time. If this keeps up we will make it in by Saturday. Wheel kicks quite a bit and when we don't watch it we get quite a jolt.

December 4

Wind changed to NE; 96 miles to go at noon. Really dangerous waters. Passed through the wreckage of another ship. Patched main and repaired leech, ready to set in a.m.

December 5

Quite a busy day. Between 4 and 8 this a.m. our watch lowered the foresail. Between noon and this afternoon it was our watch again. We jibed over twice and set up some slack rigging. Caught a shark at 6:30. Blow hit us at 10:30. Took in outer jib, staysail, jigger and main. Very dark nights this week, which makes it dangerous to walk across the deckload, which has been shifted and torn up by the seas. Saw a patrol plane.

Sunday, December 6

In sight of land all day. Saw 4 or 5 ships and were only about 5 miles off Durban when darkness caught us, so we headed back to sea. Captain didn't think it was Durban because he could see no lights, forgetting about the blackout. In his instructions it told of a flashing light, very dim, that could be seen 10 miles. We were about 18 miles off so I was asked to go up the foremast via the hoops to check on the light. I did and found it.

December 7

Becalmed at 8 a.m. Looked like we would not make it in today. But, lo and behold, here came a tug that had been sent for us. Towed us in to anchor by noon. First thing we heard was that the *Star of Scotland* was sunk between Cape Town and Brazil. It had the same rig as ours, and left the week before us. Got mail from home. Really was good to hear from the folks back home.

*   *   *   *

Tango remained in Durban more than six months for discharge of her lumber cargo, repairs and loading of a cargo of coal for delivery in Santos, Brazil. Negotiations for her sale to a Portuguese investor were completed in New York and the vessel was to have been delivered to the new owner in Santos. Meanwhile, the crew enjoyed some limited rest and relaxation, and several original members, including Fred Bitte, paid off to return to the States.

Archie McPhee's log picks up with the departure of the vessel for Santos, a voyage never completed.

Chapter 13

Roughest of All

By Archie McPhee only. He started writing June 27.

Tuesday, June 12, 1943

I wasn't going to record this trip, but things have been so damned miserable that I want some record for use for future reference when I go to spin yarns to the latest citizens of Portland, Oregon. There are now only three of us left of the original deck crew.

Present crew list:
Captain, Carl D. Gundersen
Mate, Peter Holt
2nd Mate and Bos'n, Hans Moller

Starboard watch:
McPhee, A.B., original member
Kaplan, A.B., delegate, original crew
Cheney, A.B., promoted from O.S., original crew
Joseph P. Brown (Paddy, Irishman from Londonderry)
John Maddison, O.S., South African from Durban

Port watch:
Ollie Lindbergh, A.B., Finland
Johann (Strauss) Ferruna, A.B., South African
Harold Dahl, A.B., from Norway
John B. Sampson, A.B., American
Harry Pearce, O.S., Southampton, England
Cook, James Maxwell, Australian
Messman, Charles Sparks, South African
Radio Operator, Eugene W. Luce, Nebraska, original

Carpenter, Richard Berlin, Seattle
Tango, wire-haired Scotch terrier

We finally sailed from Durban at 4 o'clock on June 12, after having spent 6 months and 6 days in that port. By 5:30 the tug had us out far enough to set sails. It already was dark, but a half moon gave us plenty of light to see by. It was a really lovely night. Set all sails but the driver. Logging between 4 and 5 knots.

June 13
Our troubles began. Becalmed with a heavy swell. On the trip down we had a deckload, which kept us from rolling. Now we are loaded heavy with coal and the least little swell makes us roll. With no wind the swell rolled us around for about 12 hours. Just about slapped the sails and rigging to pieces.

June 14
Blow hit us about 6 p.m. and, because of the beating to the rigging the day before, it started to go on us. First, the flying jib went, then a boom lift and a boom tackle strap on the spanker broke and we had to take it in. She was shipping big seas, with the seas going right over us. Lucky no one was lost. Pearce, O.S., almost got it. He was knocked off his feet and washed back and forth across the deck three or four times before someone grabbed him. The foresail went and we really took a beating getting it in as that was where the worst seas were breaking over the rail. By this time we were a tired, soaking wet bunch. And to top it off, our quarters were all flooded out. Boy, did I feel sorry for myself. We were on deck all day and all night.

June 15
Spent most of the day bailing water and clearing up wreckage of the sails. Another calm, so we lowered the rest of the sails.

June 16

Bent on the spare foresail. All hands on deck all day for the job.

June 17

Nice wind in a.m., so started setting sail at 4:30, but it turned into a gale by noon. Another day of misery, I was soaking wet from noon until midnight. We lost the outer jib and mizzen. The gaff of the mizzen wouldn't come down from the rigging and banged around up there until it knocked loose a backstay and one of the stays of the mizzen's main rigging. Worked in water up to our necks to get them secured.

June 18

In dangerous waters. Most of us are sleeping with our clothes on. Lowered sails twice and set them once today. Only headway we made was from a 3-knot current we had with us.

June 19

Reefed the fore and jigger and set them. Had to take in the fore because she was tearing the reef cringle which was drawn a little too tight. I got a good shaking sitting on the boom to patch it.

June 20

Out over a week and have made only 200 miles in the right direction and had to lose five sails to do it. 'Tis midwinter here with short days and lots of squalls, while in Portland the roses are blooming.

June 21

Set the fore and jigger by moonlight at 2:30 this a.m. Passed two lighted hospital ships at 4 a.m. An odd sight to see ships lit up now. Nice wind, ran about 5 knots all day.

June 22

Started to repair the main. Figure it will take at least two weeks. Have to take out one width of canvas and releech it. Steady wind and quiet sea.

June 23

Wind died down and we had to lower all sails. I spent the afternoon patching the inner jib. A little wind is coming up now, so we will probably be setting sail before midnight.

June 24

Set sails at 2:30 this a.m. Good wind, made 4 to 5 all day. Big row with captain over salt beef. It was rotten and we refused to eat it. Captain was the only man on the ship to eat any and claimed it was good. Two barrels went over the side tonight, the rest later. We have a large convoy of albatross and Cape Horn pigeons.

June 25

Becalmed this a.m. Nice warm day, worked without our shirts. Spotted a patrol plane at noon. We are only 70 miles offshore. In good position in case we have to take to lifeboats. Worked on the outer jib and took in the rest of the wreckage of the mizzen that had tangled in the rigging. This included the radio aerial. The radio is out of commission. We sure have tough luck with the cooks aboard here. The one we have now is sick with ulcers and if he gets worse he will not be able to work. One of the fellows has broken out with VD.

June 26

Changed to starboard tack at 1 a.m. Heading for N.W., making about 4 knots. Tore a good-sized hole in the staysail. I got the job of patching it. Getting to be an old timer when the Captain lets me do as much sewing as I have done lately. Had about ten whales playing around the ship all forenoon. When they blow on the windward side and we get a whiff of it we are reminded of a glue factory. Kaplan and the Captain had a big row about the food today. Captain got so mad he wanted to put Kaplan in irons.

June 27

We ran into a blow about 4 p.m. The only sail we could get in was the flying jib. By that time it was blowing so hard they were afraid to take in any more because the sails would whip themselves to pieces as they came down. The next best thing was to steer by the wind which gives the least pressure on the sails. The wind reached a velocity of about 60 m.p.h. and then things started to happen. First, the spanker went, tore itself all to hell. We worked with it a couple of hours. Then the big seas, which went clear over the decks sometimes, started knocking stuff free of lashings. Four oil drums, a grindstone, end of a cargo boom, smokestack of the donkey room, and took lines off the pin rails. Everybody was soaked from head to foot and earned his trip's wages every time he crossed the deck. All these things had to be lashed. Then a couple of stays came loose and they had to be secured. Moller and Cheney hurt their legs when they were thrown by the seas. It had been all hands until midnight. The wind seemed to die down about 11 p.m. The winds at sea usually change at 11 p.m. and 2 a.m. if they are going to.

June 28

At 2 a.m. the wind came up stronger than ever and the seas got heavier. We were taking them over the poop, which we had seldom done before. Our quarters were flooded out, stuff in our drawers got soaking wet. Movement of the ship got our roof loose so she leaked. Then it was all hands, for the inner jib stay broke and the staysail carried away. About this time I was feeling sorry for myself and wondering why I had to take a sailing ship when there are so many nice steamships. We managed to get both of the sails in. They were over the side. Got about an hour's rest. About 6 the foresail went and that was a real job. It knocked the smokestack loose and almost broke the liferaft adrift. Only a cold breakfast because we were rolling so bad the cook couldn't keep anything on the stove. All the rigging had slackened during the night and we had to go around and set it with the seas breaking over us. Bailed out our quarters and under the foc'sle head, which was a mess. Everything was washed off the shelves and was being washed around by seas coming through the hawse pipes, which we blocked time after time. The seas would knock the plugs loose each time. We had a chance to go below for a couple of hours but the seas were so heavy sometimes we were rolling almost 45 degrees. It was impossible to stay in a bunk. At 5 o'clock the jigger went. We just cut it loose and let the shreds go over the side. That meant 9 sails out of our 11 which went. The only ones left were the driver, which never had been set, and the flying jib, which usually is the first we take in.

June 29

The wind died down at 4 a.m. and the sea was pretty quiet by 8 a.m. We have to make an emergency port. Captain decided on Cape Town. Thinks he might get the sails of the *Commodore*, which had been rigged down into a store ship. We had about 300 miles to go and it is pretty rough. This is where the winds and currents of the Indian Ocean and Atlantic meet. Our watch repaired the staysail and set it and the flying jib this p.m.

June 30

Outer jib stay gave way, and the inner jib was already gone, so all the weight of the jibboom was on the flying jib. I had to spend 2½ hours aloft to repair it and two blocks and make the stay fast. Sitting there with the ship rolling was a thrill, a feeling the Jantzen Beach roller coaster couldn't duplicate. We cleared the wreckage of the torn sail of the jigger and started to take in the driver sail to move it to the jigger, but the seas and wind got so heavy we had to quit. About 4 p.m. three bolts on the crossbar of the steering gear sheared off. We had to put another relieving tackle on it and

Sea washing over the deck during Indian Ocean storm. (From McPhee collection.)

Captain Gundersen and Archie McPhee at broken steering wheel in Indian Ocean. (Cheney Photo. From McPhee collection.)

a couple of turnbuckles. As bad a condition as this ship is in, the Captain has changed his mind and is going to try to make it to Santos.

July 1

We are really in it now—60-foot-high waves and an 80-knot wind. The only sail we had to put up was the staysail and the wind got it about 11 a.m. The steam pipes on deck are all torn up. The puddin spar for the starboard lifeboat was broken. Six barrels got adrift on deck but the sea was so heavy we could not lash them down, so just cut holes in them and when they emptied the seas took them overboard. The Captain has finally decided we couldn't make it to Santos and now wants to head back to Durban. To protect himself, he wants all of us to sign the log we think the ship unseaworthy for the trip. We agree to this, for the rigging is all going haywire and the canvas is rotten because the sails were not taken care of properly in port. The ship has an exceptionally fine hull and really rides heavy seas nicely. Everybody is disgusted and fed up with the ship and dirty weather. This is the worst weather most of the fellows have ever seen. Got some good pictures of the storm. In one hour after I wrote that last bit at 6:55 p.m., a 10-foot sea broke over the poop from the rear. Pearce and Lindbergh were on the wheel. The sea knocked Pearce right through the wheel, breaking a third of it out, and it is a sturdy, brass-bound hardwood wheel. It threw Lindbergh right over the rail into the rigging. He was lucky he wasn't overboard. Pearce was unconscious for half an hour and is in the hospital with chest and back injuries. This same sea went right through into the galley, flooded out the stove and took everything off the table and shelves, and half-drowned the cook. The seas and wind reached their worst about 8 p.m. and the sea must have been about 80 feet high. The only thing we could do was to run with the sea or get battered to pieces. We figured we were traveling about 8 knots without a sail up. It was in a southeast direction, just the opposite of where we want to go.

July 2

Sea and wind started quieting down about 2 a.m. By noon things were pretty good. Foremast has started to crack just below the main rigging. We spent the morning trying to repair the wheel as best we could, and also repaired and patched the staysail. Still too rough to shift the jigger or try to repair any of the other sails.

July 3

This is a red letter day, for we finally got the mainsail repaired and up. Heading for Durban with about 400 miles to go. All hands on deck all day repairing sails, as the sea was calm and we now have a fair wind for Durban. I got to work on the inner jib by myself. Put in five patches and about a fathom of herring-bone stitches.

Sunday, July 4

What a way to spend the Fourth of July! This year, the Cape of Good Hope, last year off Cape Horn. The peak halyard severed at 7 a.m. All hands on deck from 7 a.m. until 7:30 p.m. The port watch worked on the main and our watch made a homeward bound job of patching the foresail and double-reefed it. Set it about 3:30. Then the whole crew worked on the main. We had it set by 7:00. And just as we started to clear up the lines, the peak halyard, which was a brand new line we had just rove in, parted and dropped the peak again so we had to take it in. It was very disappointing after working all day on a holiday and on our watch below and have our day's labor go in five minutes. The only thing that made the day stand out as a holiday was that some of the fellows had saved a few bottles of whiskey, brandy and wine. We are now two degrees farther north and it makes quite a difference in the weather.

July 5

More tough luck today. The foresail started to tear along the leech and by the reef cringle so we had to take it in about

2 p.m. Set it and then had to take it in about 9 p.m. for it started to tear again. If these sails keep tearing this way, I will be a full-fledged sailmaker by the time we get to port. Had a big school of whales playing about the ship today. About 300 miles to go at noon. Up to 34 deg. south and it is quite a bit warmer.

July 6
Practically becalmed until about 4 p.m. and now the wind has shifted from SE to NE so we might go to Port Elizabeth or East London instead of Durban, as we don't have enough sails left to buck a current and headwind. Repaired the main today and started to put the sail from the driver up on the jigger, but the Captain changed his mind and we had to put it back. Half a day's work for naught. Our dog has picked up a couple of odd habits. He thinks he can fight the sea and as long as the seas that are coming over aren't too big he runs at them and bites at the salt water. When the seas get too big he just goes into hiding. When there is no water on deck he just chases back and forth the length of the deck as fast as he can run, thinking he can catch one of the albatross or Cape Horn pigeons that soar around the ship. Saw shark, dolphins and whales today. One of the whales spurted higher than any I have seen before, 15 or 20 feet, I reckon. Pearce, the fellow who got knocked through the wheel, was feeling good enough to get up today.

July 7
Instead of changing course and heading for Port Elizabeth, we have hove-to and are waiting for the wind to change. We can use any wind but the NE wind we have now. We had a major catastrophe today. The radio operator broke the spring on the phonograph. The phonograph was given us by the American and Canadian Club and is the only luxury and source of entertainment on board. We managed to scrape up a few good records. I got Gene Autry in "Back in the Saddle." I can just imagine how John and Tom would like to hear that

one. Also, I got "Roll Along Kentucky Moon," "It Makes No Difference Now," and "Corn Silk" by Guy Lombardo. Nice weather with a quiet sea. Feels good to be able to go around without seaboots and oilskins for a change.

July 8
The wind changed to SW and was fair for us, but the barometer started to fall fast, so we just stayed hove-to nursing the sails we have left. We have only the staysail up. It helps to steer. Blow hit us at 4 p.m. and it is a humdinger. One sea came over the poop just before 6 p.m. and almost washed the mate overboard. He was saved by the rigging. Making two or three knots in the right direction without any sails up.

July 9
Storm is still raging. Decks are continually awash. One is lucky if he can go from fore to aft or aft to fore without getting soaked. Staysail was ripped to shreds about 7 a.m. It has been patched quite a few times this trip, though, so we expected it. In the 28 days I have been out this time since leaving Durban, I have seen more really bad weather than all the rest of the time I have been to sea. The other fellows with lots more time at sea are saying the same thing. So far, it has been just one storm after another, and two of them as bad as they come. At noon we had 256 miles to go. Wouldn't take long on a steamship, but on this thing it could be days, weeks, or months.

July 10
My birthday. This year off the Cape of Good Hope, last year off Cape Horn. I was awakened to go on watch this morning by the radio operator, Strauss and Ollie singing "Happy Birthday." Storm had subsided by 4 a.m. and we had a nice day with 217 miles to go by noon. The wind shifted back to the north again so we are laying hove-to. The boom lift on the starboard side of the driver carried away last night.

179

Lucky we were steering from the port side or the man on the wheel would have been beaned. To save money, they renewed only about a third of the lines and halyards and the old ones are getting so rotten it doesn't take much to break them. I have just made up my mind to pay-off if they don't rig her out better than before this time. Saw a large school of whales today. The war has curtailed the whaling industry to practically nothing. I guess that is why there are so many whales about.

July 11
One month out today and we are only 227 miles from our port of departure. Wind is still from NW so we are hove-to. Lost 10 miles in the last 24 hours. Boom lift chafed a couple of holes in the foresail, so I spent part of my Sunday off patching it. The carpenter and I fixed the spring of the phonograph and it was nice to hear some music again. Very large swells. Two of them came unusually close together about 10:30. The first one rolled us in position to take the second one and it came about 10 feet above the rail. It flooded the carpenter room, the radio operator, the hospital, and the cook and messman's room. Ollie and the cook had a big row today. The cook is not a cook and can put out only canned food. So Ollie told him to have his bags ready to go ashore as soon as we docked.

July 12
The wind shifted to SW so we set the inner jib, the foresail and main. Doing about 2 knots with 235 miles to go at noon. Another catastrophe occurred when the ancient mariner wound up the phonograph and broke the spring again.

July 13
174 miles to go at noon. The wind died down at 2:30 p.m. and we got some large swells that flapped the sails so much the foresail tore in two places. So we took it and the main in. Have only the inner jib and flying jib up now. Fixed the phonograph again today. Was satisfied to find it was a new

break in the spring and not the one we fixed the other day. Nice moonlight night.

July 14

Wind came up strong from the NE, so we set the main. Not making much time because our course is too close to the wind. 140 miles to go at noon. Captain very happy today, the dog caught a big rat. Dahl and I patched the foresail this a.m.

July 15

At 11:30 last night, ten minutes after I made yesterday's entry, the main started tearing in two places and we had to lower it. At 12:30 a.m., just before we turned in, we broke the phonograph spring again. The spring is getting as temperamental as the sails. We fixed both the spring and sail during our afternoon watch, and also put a reef in the main and set it by 4:30. 155 miles to go at noon. Still NE wind but it should be changing to a southerly by tomorrow. A bunch of yellowtails were playing around the ship and they broke three lines and none were caught. Carpenter and messboy have tonsillitis. This a.m. the mate didn't want to tackle reefing and repairing the main with his watch. Said it should be all hands in the afternoon, but when we came on deck we told them to go below, that we could handle it, and that we did. Full moon tonight.

July 16

120 miles to go at noon. Practically becalmed. What little wind we have has gone back to northerly, which we don't want. Had to wear ship three times today—that is changing tack. A big shark was hanging around most of the day, but nobody could catch him. Quite a few of the new fellows had never been close to an albatross and they were having no luck trying to catch them with the triangle, so I put the McPhee system to work and caught two Cape pigeons and two albatross for them with my bare hands in about 15 minutes. The new fellows had quite a time getting their pictures taken with

the birds. The dog got his nose bitten a few times, then decided to leave the birds alone. Warm day—roamed the decks barefooted and without shirts. Amidship the deck had so much water that it is slimy and green, making it hard to keep footing. We have been 80 to 100 miles offshore for the last 10 days and have seen no air patrol or patrol boats. Suggests inadequate patrol to us.

July 17

140 miles to go at noon. We lost 20 miles. NE wind and NW current, which are taking us south and west. The farther west we drift the stronger the southerly current. It gets as strong as 7 knots. The tides and currents are stronger under a full or new moon, which we now are having. Caught a shark at 7 p.m. Only a six-footer. The little pilot fish was still clinging to him when we brought the shark aboard. It was supposed to be good luck to have a shark's tail nailed on the end of the bowsprit. We are going to nail it up tomorrow and look for the best. The dog is keeping a steady lookout by the shark. He won't leave it—keeps walking around it, watching it and going up for an occasional sniff. Started to blow about 10 p.m.

July 18

Blew hard enough by 4 a.m. to start tearing the main, so it was taken in. By 6 a.m. there was a heavy swell but no wind. The ship started rolling, causing the foresail to flap pretty bad. It has broken the boom tackle straps and then started tearing along the leech, so it came in. Half an hour later the wind came up from the SW where we wanted it, but no sails until morning. We will lose about 60 miles by not having any sails up. Captain is on edge, made the fellows take in three fish lines they had over the poop. He claimed they were holding back the ship. We had another argument with him over the salt beef and pork. It is absolutely rotten and he got mad when the fellows were using it for bait. The shark was cut up and distributed amongst us today. Pearce skinned it and is going to have a jacket made of it. Ollie is going to make a cane of the backbone. It has three sets of teeth. The rest of us got those. The tail is nailed to the bowsprit. 142 miles to go at noon. Lost only two miles in the last 24 hours.

July 19

It was a good thing the fore and main were down, because we had a real blow today. One big sea about 2 p.m. picked up the forward lifeboat and lifted it to the roof of the foc'sle. This same sea flooded the engine room. Hope it hasn't damaged the machinery. 90 miles to go at 3 p.m. The sea and wind are with us and we are doing as much as 5 knots with only the inner jib set. We have made more distance running before the sea and wind without any sails up than we had made under sail this trip. We just missed a couple of water spouts. One of them had five fingers. If we had got caught by one of them it might have capsized us. Had a heavy rainstorm at 4 p.m. that beat the wind and sea down quite a bit.

July 20

Sea and wind quieted down by midnight and changed to NE. At 6 a.m. a convoy passed us. One of the escorting destroyers inquired where we were going and then left before the Captain had a chance to ask them to send us a tug. Dahl and I turned to at 7 a.m. and had the fore and main sails repaired by 10:30. Then along came two patrol vessels, Nos. 162 and 267, converted fishing trawlers. No. 162 gave us a towline, but it broke on the first strain. Then 267 gave us his line, first shooting with a gun. Six heaving lines attached to it and then bigger lines until we got their wire, which was to hook over two anchor chains. Just as we got their wire alongside, the line parted and they had about 600 feet of their wire hanging straight down under them. They had to pull it in by hand, a tough job. They shot us another line with a series of lines graduating up to a new 8-inch mooring which didn't break. We finally were under tow by 4 p.m. with fully 50 miles to go to Durban. No. 267 is towing and 162 is circling us continually. It is a bright moonlight night and it feels good to have a tow and escort. The fellows are intending to take up a tarpaulin muster, if we get a draw, to buy the boys on the 267 a case of whiskey, because we really created a lot of work for them and their wages run only about 20 cents a day.

July 21

In port and safe.

Chapter 14

Fire at Sea

The second visit to Durban proved to be another long idleness—more than eight months. The time was late 1943 and early 1944. The war in Europe was in full bloom and Americans and British were massing in England for an invasion of Normandy to begin a big push of Germans back into their own territory. The Axis already had been expelled from Africa and the Russians were pushing hard in western Russia and Poland. U-boats were still working around the tip of South Africa and poky old sailing vessels like the *Tango* were sitting ducks.

This made the crew of the *Tango* fidgety and restless. Several of the original members wanted to go home and drew their pay. One of them was Hans Moller, the second mate.

Captain Gundersen called Archie McPhee into his spare little office and offered him the second mate's job. McPhee also was getting tired of his adventure and told the Captain he was ready to go home. But the Captain respected the young man's ability and hard work on the ship and insisted on him staying. McPhee informed the Captain the only way he could act as second mate was to be allowed a free hand and to abide by his union's rules. The Captain agreed and McPhee stayed.

Meanwhile, Peter Holt, the original first mate, also paid-off and found a passage back to New York. A new mate was signed—one C. Heydenrich, who claimed Norwegian citizenship, a claim that later proved to be questioned. McPhee and Heydenrich roomed together.

"When he was sober he was a pretty good guy," said McPhee later. "But when he came in drunk it was a different story, and he was hard to get along with. We soon found he was not a sailing ship man and I had to take over most of his duties. The Captain agreed to this."

While the rest of the crew amused themselves ashore as sailors do, McPhee was invited to escort local ladies to parties and dances, wined and dined at no great expense to himself.

"And I behaved myself," he declared. "I was back in the ship every night."

As second mate, McPhee proposed to his crew that if they would turn-to and do a usual day's work between 8 a.m. and noon, they could have the rest of the day off and go ashore. The men liked this arrangement and did the necessary ship-keeping in four hours, compared with all day or more as was usual.

One day Captain Gundersen arrived back on the noon shore boat and met his crew leaving for town. He stormed to his new second mate. "What is the meaning of this, letting these men off at noon?" he burst out.

"I took him about the ship and pointed out the newly-polished compass binnacle, shining as never before, the dried and mended sails, the decks scrubbed clean, and everything in its place," McPhee explained later. "That satisfied the Old Man and he let me run the ship my way."

During this long lay-up, McPhee had the men scrape and pound off the heavy layer of barnacles and sea life on the hull. The vessel was light after its coal cargo had been discharged and was drawing only eight feet, so most of the barnacles were within easy reach. Removal of this debris resulted in better going when *Tango* next went to sea.

Several new faces were added to the crew before it sailed for Lourenco Marques, Portuguese East Africa. The new crew was more international than ever. It included seven Americans, two South Africans, two Finns, two Norwegians, one Swede, one Englishman, one Irishman, and a Latvian. Added also was a German dachshund dog and an alley cat. Cheney named the dog "Bilgewater."

Only five members of the original list remained: the Captain, McPhee, Luce, Kaplan, and Cheney.

With 1,500 tons of coal in the lower holds as ballast, *Tango* sailed February 9, 1944, for Lourenco Marques, about 320 miles up the east coast of Africa, to be delivered to a new owner and to receive a new cargo. The seven-day voyage was made in yet-dangerous waters. While the fire in Europe was being contained, there were sparks elsewhere.

So it was on the *Tango*. On the second day out, the men noted smoke and gases issuing from two hatches. Two days later the fumes were stronger, and by the fifth day they were in the quarters and made sleeping nearly impossible.

"With smoke coming out of two ventilators, we looked like a two-stacker," mused McPhee.

The Captain radioed to British authorities for instructions and was advised to get to Lourenco Marques as quickly as possible, sail up the St. Mary's River until the ship touched a mud bank, then open the sea valves and sink the ship on the mud to extinguish the fire. A tug was ordered to meet the ship and tow it into port, where the ship was sunk deep enough to flood the coal cargo and put out the flames. A day later, pumps were installed to discharge the water and refloat the ship. The coal was unloaded and offered for sale, but no buyers showed up. Much of the coal finally was given to a school, according to McPhee.

Cause of the fire was suspected to be incendiary, and the new mate, Heydenrich, was suspected of sabotage. He was known to have visited German sympathizers in Durban and he always had money not obtained from the ship. He associated with Germans in the city. A week after the *Tango* arrived in Lourenco Marques, the mate was arrested and charged with sabotage by tossing inflammable pencils into the coal. It was determined he was a native German, but reared in Norway. He had strong German sympathies. He finally was taken to England for trial, according to the word given the crew.

The day after the *Tango* arrived, an international battle was waged between three crew members and a dozen local police. "We were knocking the hell out of them until they got reinforcements from a group of civilians," McPhee explained. "Then we broke and ran. Americans were not well-liked there."

The following day, McPhee learned some of the police were in a hospital and complaints had been filed against an unknown American sailor. "I laid low for a couple of weeks," he added.

But, let's let McPhee tell about the run up the coast and the Lourenco Marques sojourn as he logged it in February, 1944:

Wednesday, February 9, 1944

This is the big day, we are finally sailing again. Tugs towed us out 7 miles, dropped us at 1:30 p.m. Ship is riding nicely. We have only 1,500 tons of coal in ballast and are not drawing much water. The ballast is well-trimmed and the ship is not rolling much. We are under full sail by 2:30 p.m. Took in the driver at 6 p.m. Steering by the wind and making 6 knots. She will be plenty fast with a fair wind. Cleaning the bottom has helped a lot. Several changes in the crew:

Capt. Carl Gundersen, U.S.
1st Mate, C. Heydenrich, Norwegian
2nd Mate, A. McPhee, Oregonian
Cook, Harry Morgan, South African
Messboy, Symington, South African
Sparks, E. Luce, U.S.
Carpenter, R. Berlin, U.S.

Port watch:
A.B. Ollie Lindbergh, Finnish
A.B. Carl Below, Swedish
A.B. Arne Kaasinen, Finnish
A.B. Ralph Sampson, U.S.
O.S. Harry Pearce, English

Starboard watch:

O.S. Arne Kaasa, Norwegian
A.B. Joe Kaplan, U.S.
A.B. Ira Cheney, U.S.
A.B. Jack Binder, Latvian
A.B. Paddy Brown, Irishman
Dachshund dog and an alley cat.

Our coal ballast has started to give off gas and smoke and we are afraid of fire.

February 10

Still NE wind and we are staying as close to it as possible, even though we are making as much as 8½ knots. Took in the flying jib at 12 M. Nice clear moonlight night. Fire in the ballast isn't getting any worse. Saw flying fish and porpoises. Playing deck golf for recreation.

February 11

Took in main, jigger, and spanker to slow down until we get a fair wind. Captain can't trust the mate with handling sails, so our watch gets most of it. Fire in the ballast is a little worse. Saw a dozen flares. Not being a lifeboat type, we didn't investigate. Mate has been torpedoed in these waters twice in last year, so he was quite upset and paced the deck all night.

February 12

Passed a hospital ship at 12:30 a.m. Wind changed to SW at 2 a.m. It is now fair and we are doing 8 knots with only three sails up. Foresail broke this a.m., had to take it in. It was torn between the single and double reefs, so we double reefed and reset it. Set the main at 9 a.m. Just as we got it up, the throat halyard parted and down she came, tearing a couple of small holes in herself. We patched it and rove in a new halyard and set it again. We were on deck from 4 a.m. till 12 M.

February 13

Foresail went and we had to take in the remnants. Main tore, was patched and set again, and we had to take it in six hours later. Had to send fellows into the hatches to get scraps of wood. It was dangerous because of the gas from the coal. The carpenter claimed he could fire his boiler only with oil, but we got up 130 pounds pressure in 1½ hours. His diesel engine, which is used to get up steam for the donkey boiler, is haywire. The fire is getting worse and the fumes from it are getting into the quarters, making it hard to sleep.

February 14
Main tore again and had to be taken in. then the second mate, Yours Truly, had to sew for six hours to patch it. Captain came and asked me to sew it myself because he wanted to be sure it was a good job. He gave me eight hours overtime for it. We set sail and the patch was perfect. Boastfully put. Came in sight of the lighthouse where we pick up the pilot for Lourenco Marques, but couldn't make it by dark, so we hove-to all night outside waiting for the morning. Fire in the holds really bad. Had to sleep on deck.

February 15
Becalmed at 6 this a.m. so we wired for a tug, which arrived at 11. Took in all our sails and prepared the hatches for the firemen to get to the fire. Some of the fellows went ashore and got into trouble. Sparks was in jail and will be there at least a week, and has been fined $125.

February 16
Flooded the ship to put out the fire. Went ashore today. Ollie, Brown and I got in a fight with four Portuguese police, knocked the hell out of them when eight more came up. We were getting the best of them until some civilians pitched in and started to help them, so we fought our way out and took to our heels and all of us got away. Carpenter got hit over the head and rolled. They took everything except his shoes. When he came to and tried to get back to the ship, he was arrested and fined $25 for being nude on the streets. There is a very strong dislike for Americans here.

February 17

Pumping the water out today. There is going to be an investigation because the fire was on top of the coal so it had to be set. Spontaneous combustion sets in underneath where it can generate its heat. Found out today that we put the police in the hospital and they had complaints out against me, but don't know who I am. Will have to lay low for a couple of weeks.

Sunday, February 20

Captain told me today the mate is under suspicion of sabotage, because of having visited German sympathizers and also because of some remarks he made. His every move is being followed and they are checking on him and his friends in Durban. We have been catching a lot of fish, of every size and shape, including prawns and crab.

Thursday, February 24

Mate was arrested today, but we can get no details about it. We are going to have to wait for the new crew to come and they haven't left Portugal yet, and it is better than a month's trip to here. I have the ship in very good condition now. Everything is freshly painted and all our rigging is in good order. The mate hadn't been on a sailing ship before, so I was doing most of his work, which was to lay out the work and decide what should be done to keep the rigging in top condition.

Tuesday, February 29

Taking life easy; just having the men dry the sails and wash down the decks. Our main recreations are deck golf, fishing, swimming, and a couple of fellows are building small boats. Sparks is out of jail now. We will be darned lucky if no one gets malaria as there are lots of mosquitoes and no netting.

Sunday, March 5

Took a chance and went ashore today. Brown, Cheney, the carpenter and I took a train about 30 miles inland to Villa

Luisa and a boat trip from there about 20 miles up the river. It was very interesting. We saw several herds of hippos and got within a couple of feet of them; lots of crocodiles, some species of boks and other animals too far from the river to distinguish, and some native kraals. On the way back, Brown got drunk at the R.R. station and broke a window on the train as he was getting off. He tried to run for it, but they caught him and it cost him $25 for a $5 window.

March 6
Mate was sent to England to the Norwegian government. We were told it was very serious and he probably would be shot. Still taking it easy. Wish they would have some one from ashore until the other crew comes and sends us home.

Thursday, March 16
Most of the crew is to be sent to Durban Monday, so we started giving the sails a good drying today.

March 17
Finished drying the sails today. Lindbergh, Kaasinen, Kaasa, Binder, Berlin, Morgan, Symington, Brown, Pearce and Samson paid off this afternoon, so I had to go on a big party with them. They all had over $500 so it was mostly champagne. We had the American Vice Consul, Hunt, a very fine fellow, drinking with us.

March 18
Went alongside to discharge our coal. Had to give it away as none would buy it. I was a very busy boy, for the only ones aboard were the Captain, Cheney, Kaplan, and myself. We had to handle the tug's lines and then I had to run the diesel to take up the anchor for the carpenter had been paid-off. They gave us a few natives to help tie up because we have no machinery for our lines. Have to have all the coal discharged before we can get the Veritas surveyors report which the new owners want before they will accept the ship. They are afraid the fire may have warped some of the beams or burned the

flooring. Quite a few townspeople have been walking down to the ship. Because of the large number of pro-Nazis around here, we have orders to allow no visitors aboard.

Monday, March 20

Crew left on the morning train. We went down to see them off. Sure wished we were going with them. Seems quite lonesome aboard the ship with only four of us left with the Captain. Hired an Indian cook and two negroes to serve and keep the quarters clean.

Thursday, March 23

Still discharging. Having quite a bit of fun with natives working in the mess. We have been giving them our old clothes. It is very hot here and when they go ashore they wear some heavy overcoats we gave them and worn-out work gloves so they feel very proud.

The one who takes care of my room saw Ferne's picture and, through the watchman who speaks their language, asked me how much I would have to pay for a wife like that in the States. He was astounded when I told him, "Nothing," and he went on to explain that he was trying to save some money to buy cows to trade for a 9-year-old girl he wanted for a wife.

Chapter 15

Lourenco Marques and Lisbon

After the ten crew members drew their pay and departed March 20, the five remaining—Captain Gundersen, McPhee, Luce, Kaplan, and Cheney—waited for five months until the Portuguese crew arrived to relieve them. McPhee said it was a long, lonesome wait because the men were more or less confined to the ship. They did not allow visitors and sightseers to come aboard because there was too much sympathy in Lourenco Marques for the German cause.

Captain Gundersen hired an Indian cook to prepare meals and two black natives to handle housekeeping duties. The Americans busied themselves with minimal shipkeeping duties and entertained themselves with deck golf, fishing over the side, swimming near the ship, and standing guard at the gangplank.

The captain obtained some old sails from the former American schooner *Commodore*, which had been cut down to a storage barge, and McPhee and his men used them for patching torn *Tango* sails.

During the past year, the sale of the *Tango* to a Portuguese shipowner had been progressing slowly. Records of the National Archives in Washington, D.C., show that the *Tango* was first registered with the U.S. Department of Commerce March 4, 1942, with New York as home port. The vessel then was at St. Helens, Oregon, being made ready for the Cape Horn trip.

Transatlantic Navigation Co., Inc., of New York, filed an application with the U.S. Maritime Commission for permission to sell the *Tango* to Julio Ribeiro Campos, of Oporto, Portugal, and the order was approved December 23, 1943. No

Tango *high and almost dry in harbor at Lourenco Marques. (From McPhee collection.)*

price was reported. The American registration was surrendered June 13, 1944, when the ship was officially sold and transferred to the Portuguese flag at Lourenco Marques. It had been there four months, waiting, and was destined to remain there a year longer.

Campos renamed the ship *Cidade do Porto*, after his home city. Another Portuguese owner soon became interested in the vessel and purchased it from Campos, reputedly for $430,000, a princely sum for an aging ship with a varied past and questionable future. But the World War was still going strong and old shipping hulls had value. The vessel lay in Lourenco Marques for nearly a year awaiting a charter and loading orders. A Portuguese government commission regulating the cotton and wool trade took over the ship to haul a cargo of Mozambique cotton to Portugal, but this cargo failed to materialize.

When the five Americans were about to leave the ship for home, they had some left-over worn clothes to give away. McPhee related that he decked out one small native housekeeper with some of the smallest trousers and a shirt he could find, a big old overcoat, a hat, pair of gloves and boots.

"When he went ashore, he looked like a Chinese laundry," McPhee said. "The temperature was 110 degrees in the shade, but the man was happy and proud. Another native came and wanted a similar outfit, but all I had left was some old oilskins and other stuff. He was disappointed."

After the Portuguese crew arrived, the Americans split up. Captain Gundersen, McPhee and Cheney took a coastal steamer to Beira, Mozambique, where they booked passage on an American Liberty ship to the U.S. Others returned on other vessels.

"I got chummy with the captain of the Liberty and played cribbage with him," McPhee related. "He cheated so much I finally told him I would play according to 'West Coast rules' and I would demand double pay.

"I was up in the chart room when he was plotting courses. He said we were going to Portland. I told him that was great—Portland is my home town. But when we got to Trinidad and headed north, I pointed out that the way to Portland lay west. Then he informed me we were going to Portland, Maine—not Oregon. That was my come-down.

"From Portland, Maine, we took the train to New York, stopping at New Haven, Connecticut, where Ira's folks met him and greeted us. They were very appreciative of the attention we gave Ira during his 2½ years on the ship. Ira left us there.

"At New York, the company insisted on keeping me around for a couple of weeks while they finished up the *Tango* business. When I left for Oregon, they gave me a big, nicely wrapped package as a going-away gift. I thought it was something nice for my wife or our future home, but when I opened it on the train I found 72 small bottles of whiskey. I was not drinking and gave the bottles away to people on the train."

A year after *Tango* became *Cidade do Porto* and the Portuguese flag replaced the Stars and Strips, the Portuguese government loaded her with coal for Lobito, Angola, and she sailed August 24, 1945, from Lourenco Marques. She had a far larger crew than she carried as the *Tango*. Again, she ran into storms and heavy seas which wrecked the sails and she had to be towed into Durban to lick her wounds. She was delayed there for three months.

Underway again, the ship ran into another wrecking storm and was adrift for two weeks off the southern tip of Africa. Again she was towed into port, this time Cape Town. Here was another delay for three months for repairs. From there she was under tow all the way to Lisbon, stopping enroute at Lobito to discharge the coal cargo and to load a cargo of cotton and hides for Portugal. The war in Europe had been over for a year. Germany's U-boats and raiders were gone and the oceans again were free for commerce.

A Portuguese steamer took *Cidade do Porto* in tow August 17, 1946, and she arrived in Lisbon September 20, 34 days from Lobito. That ended her travels. She lay idle in the Tagus River for nearly two years while Portuguese authorities sought a suitable use for her. A suggestion that she be converted into a training ship for young seamen was passed over as too expensive. Again, a glut of war-built steamships and motorships had destroyed the market for old sailers. And no Robert Dollar stepped forward to save her.

Now a derelict, unloved and unwanted in the Tagus, the *Cidade do Porto* was put on the auction block April 8, 1948. She was sold to Theofilo Carvalho Duarte, whose only interest in the ship was to dismantle and scrap the stately vessel. She hadn't even made it to her home port, Oporto.

Gone she was, but not forgotten by the men associated with her during her working life, which actually was less than one-half her career of 44 years. She had spent more time waiting than working.

The handsome *Hans* filled a niche in maritime history. Launched in Glasgow, Scotland, back in 1904, she and her sister, *Kurt*, were the ultimate in fine cargo-carrying sailing vessels. They performed well and profitably for their owners during their prime days, 1904 to 1914.

The *Hans/Mary Dollar* was the gleam in Captain Robert Dollar's eyes, even while laid up in San Francisco Bay boneyards for 13 long years. Then she served an inglorious period as a floating gambling den, now named *Tango*, beyond the three-mile limit west of Los Angeles, California. She wound up her most useful career by making the desperate and successful run without motor power from Oregon to South Africa via the stormy Cape Horn route, during a vicious war and a treacherous mid-winter.

The *Hans/Mary Dollar/Tango/Cidade do Porto* had eight different owners and flew four different national flags during her 44 years.

She was one of the largest schooners in the world, the largest bald-headed schooner of her time, the second largest six-masted schooner ever built, the largest sailing ship under the American flag when she made her 22nd and final passage around Cape Horn, and she was the last large American-flag commercial sailing vessel to pass the Horn.

She deserved a better end.

Chapter 16

The Radio Operator Surfaces

After the first printing of *"Tango"* in November, 1990, the whereabouts of Gene Luce, the radio operator on the *Tango* for more than two years, became known to old friends in Oregon and to the author of this report.

Luce's cousin, Michael Cannady, of Eugene, Oregon, and his uncle, Bruce B. Cannady, of Gresham, Oregon, had read a book review published in the Portland *Oregonian* which extolled this book and they purchased three copies, one of which they sent to Gene, now retired in Seagrove, North Carolina.

Bruce Cannady telephoned the author in Portland and provided his nephew's address and phone number. That inspired a round of correspondence which resulted in Luce's reflections on the *Tango*'s voyages from the Columbia River to South Africa and in the Indian Ocean during the years Gene was on the ship.

Right off the bat, Gene corrected Archie McPhee's statement that the radio operator "was flying from New York" (May 1, 1942) to join the ship at Astoria.

> I was working the second shift at Boeing Aircraft in Seattle and also attending a radio class during the day at the YMCA. On the morning of May 1 our instructor announced he had a ridiculous call from a shipping agent at Portland who wanted a student radio operator for a sailing ship (no license required). He told them he had some men who could qualify but doubted if any were crazy enough to take it.

The instructor's doubts were unfounded, he did have one student crazy enough to jump at the chance even though he wasn't as far along in school as a number of the other students. I raised my hand and told him I would like to have the job, if he thought I could handle it. He said 'Okay, if you are sure I will call the agent back'.

I got the assignment and by 10:30 that night I was on a bus to Portland after having talked to my dad in Nebraska, then going out to Boeing to sell my tools and draw my pay. While riding on the bus all I could think of was that not in my wildest dreams did I ever think I would get a chance for adventure and travel like this, particularly at age 18 and only a few months out of high school.

The eighteen year old draft had not been enacted as yet but I had received a letter from my mother just a couple of weeks earlier asking me not to do anything foolish, like joining the army or navy since I worked in an industry that would keep me out of the services. So-oh, I called my dad at a neighbors'. He was quite shocked when I told him I was taking a sailing ship to South Africa and particularly concerned about my mother's reaction. I learned later that her first reaction was 'Oh, no he isn't' but by the next day had resigned herself to it.

After the bus ride I rented a room and spent a very sleepless couple of hours before having to get ready to meet my agents. I was there when the office opened. They thought I looked so young that one of the agents called my parents. After they finished talking I got my chance to talk to my mother, who cried, but did not try to keep me from going. After the phone conversation the agents took me to Astoria and put me on the *Tango*.

201

I did not have a radio operator's license, seaman's papers, passport or overseas shots. All I had was a photostat of my birth certificate, a very limited knowledge of radio and was anything but proficient in code. When the Coast Guard came aboard for a final inspection they looked at the radio equipment but didn't ask any questions. We sailed the same day.

Luce was born in Columbus, Nebraska, 67 years ago (1924) and grew up in Bayard, out in the "panhandle" of Nebraska, about 24 miles from Scottsbluff. These were depression days and Gene worked 40 hours a week at a dairy while attending high school. The hours were spread out over Saturday, Sunday, and before and after school on week days. One half of his monthly pay of $24 went back to the dairy to pay the milk bill for the Luce family.

My hero was Richard Halliburton (1900-1939), the adventurer, author and lecturer. I loved his books, particularly 'The Royal Road to Romance.' He had died at the age of 39 in a typhoon while attempting to sail a Chinese junk to the U.S. The girl I dated most in high school (Lois Bristol) had a heroine, Amelia Earhart, the aviatrix who disappeared in the South Pacific while trying to fly around the world. Lois later became a ferry pilot flying planes to England during the war.

Luce graduated from high school at the age of 17 and then struck out in search of adventure. With $6 in his pocket and some clothes in a suitcase he started down the highway, bound west by northwest. His parents worried. The road led him to the state of Washington where a friendly farmer stopped him near Maryhill, about 100 miles east of Portland and asked him if he could pitch hay.

I had no work clothes but I took the job for the few days it lasted at $2.50 a day with board. The farmer wrote a letter of recommendation addressed to a bar man in Moro, Oregon, and I started out again. A man driving to California picked me up and asked me to be his relief driver to San Francisco. I agreed if things didn't work out in Moro, but they did. After stopping and showing the letter to the bartender, I found myself back out in a field pitching hay by four o'clock that same afternoon. I stayed through the summer and harvest, still at $2.50 a day and board and room.

After the harvest I hitch-hiked to Portland and went to an N.Y.A. sheet metal school where I was also given the toolroom attendant's job at 50 cents an hour. Next I went to Seattle, got a job with Boeing and moved into the Y.M.C.A. I was there when Japan bombed Pearl Harbor.

Luce said he had no intention of going to sea until that moment the *Tango* job came to light. He had no time to buy clothes and had only those he wore and some in a suitcase when he went aboard the ship with no chance to get off for over three months. He had neither the thought nor materials for keeping a diary or "log" but did have a good memory.

On board he suffered a bit of sea sickness the first three days at sea, then became a "good Sailor" for the remainder of the voyage, even during extremely rough periods.

He soon became friendly with Fred Bitte, the carpenter, who had a small cabin across the alleyway from the radio shack where Luce lived. He also made friends with Archie McPhee, an outstanding member of the deck crew tending sails. Gene was the youngest man on board and got along well with Ira Cheney, an ordinary seaman and next youngest, and with Joe Kaplan, the Jewish able-bodied seaman on McPhee's watch.

Luce and Bitte better known as "Chips" had a nightly rummy game, with the understanding that the loser would buy the winner all the malted milkshakes he could drink when

Gene Luce (left) and Fred Bitte, the rummy players, on deck. (From Luce collection.)

they arrived at the first port. Gene was the overall victor. Bitte was older, a family man, obviously homesick, and though a great asset to the ship, "really didn't belong there," according to Luce. He kept more or less to himself when not busy firing the steam donkey engine for raising sails or mending other gear. "He was probably the nicest guy on board," Gene mused.

Gene, Ira, Archie and Joe formed a clique that stayed together until the vessel was sold in 1944 and continued to correspond and visit with each other for years thereafter.

> We never called Joe a Jew on shipboard although I see Archie referred to him as such in his log. I believe Archie called him "Joe" just as the rest of us did. At any rate they were great friends until Joe died.

Luce said he got along well with Captain Gundersen who regarded the young man as a special extra asset, a sort of lifeline to civilization if anything went wrong with the ship.

> During bad storms the captain didn't want me out on deck where I might get washed overboard and leave no one to send out emergency signals. The rest of the crew seemed to feel safer with "Sparks" (as all radio men are called) aboard. I didn't tell them but I felt their confidence was unfounded since I wasn't sure I was capable of sending off an emergency message.

> I helped a little on deck when the sea was calm but the captain frowned on it so I became a passenger most of the time although Archie did teach me to sew canvas and tie a number of sailor knots. I made my own canvas duffel bag and the knots I learned have kept me in good stead ever since. We didn't have the best battery charging system and the captain wanted to save the batteries for an emergency. Some of the time though I did listen to the radio and

tried to improve my code and did pick up a couple of SOSs.

One man I didn't get along with was the bos'n, Jim Burke—"Bucko Bos'n Burke" we called him. He had a little radio in his cabin, which was next to mine. It was a little battery operated radio and he kept filling in the captain with what he heard on the voice channels.

That led to one altercation I had with him. I was small (120 lbs.) and always thought I looked somewhat sissified. Because of it I guess I kind of carried a chip on my shoulder which caused me to get in to many scraps from the time I entered school until I got married.

On this occasion I had left my glasses in the cabin because I thought there might be trouble (I didn't know what I could do about it but I wanted Burke to know I wouldn't back off from him). It happened in the galley where we were drinking coffee when Burke said something that wasn't true and I called him a liar. He slapped me and I set down my cup and tied into him. It took him less than ten seconds to get me on the lower side and up against the bulkhead. He told me to take it back but in seamen's words I expressed what I thought of him and his probable ancestry. He could have laid me out with one strong punch but instead he kept cuffing me with both hands while I was hitting him in the stomach while I continued my monologue.

That went on until Chips picked up an iron skillet from the stove and said "that's enough!" Burke stopped and so did I but the next day my ears, eyes and cheeks were black and blue. That's what Archie saw the next day and mentioned in his log (July 30, 1942). I never did take it back. The only man on the ship who could have taken Burke in a knock-down, drag-out fight was Archie—that's my opinion.

Archie mentioned Burke and Angelo getting into a couple of scraps and neither were really hurt. I saw one of those. One had his fingers in the other's nose trying to rip it and the other had his fingers in his adversary's mouth trying to tear it. But the fight finally died out.

It was an odd mixture of men for a crew of only seventeen. A couple of us were young and inexperienced, a couple too old for other ships, three or four with physical disabilities, a couple "unsatisfactory citizens" whom the government would not let return to the States and most all had not been in sailing ships before. The cook had been released from jail to go along. He was not a good cook, and the messboy was no good at all. Archie mentioned that the cook threatened to jump overboard if the crew didn't quit complaining and when he didn't jump, some of the men threatened to throw him overboard. He got so he would stay in his cabin where he was safe. Even with all these personality differences we got along pretty well together.

Down in the doldrums with no wind and where the water was warm, some of the men were trying to catch an albatross. They started daring each other to jump in and catch one. I was young and without good sense so I got up on the rail and jumped in, catching an albatross by the neck and went under the water with it. I thought it would want to come back up and bring us both to the top but I soon realized that wasn't his intention. I let go of him and surfaced by myself and started swimming back to the ship. Then somebody shouted "Sparks! Sparks!" and I thought a shark was after me. I swam harder and faster to the ship which wasn't moving and they pulled me aboard. There was no shark but a couple of albatross were swimming toward me and my friends thought they would peck me. If the captain had seen me do it I would have been in for a real tongue lashing.

Chips gave a pretty good account of our rummy games. I also played cribbage with Swede Rowley, one of the ordinary seamen. He said he was so dumb he couldn't hit the deck with his hat, and he wasn't too far from being right. He was almost illiterate although he did have some comic books with him that he either read or looked at the pictures. When we played cribbage he often disagreed with me on how many of the hands should be counted. I told him to show them to his shipmates and they always agreed I was right. He finally said everyone was just siding with me and refused to play anymore.

Oh yes, the weevils. The weevils got into everything. We tried to get them out but couldn't. It got down to the point that we ate weevils and all. Many of the meals consisted of dry breakfast cereal with weevils and milk. I can't believe that neither Archie nor Chips failed to mention the weevils.

Four of us ate in the salon; the captain, mate, bos'n and I. For breakfast I would get in first and eat my cereal before they brought in the captain's mackerel or codfish. The stench was so bad I couldn't stand it. As Archie pointed out "that lousy, stinking codfish". The captain was the last to give up. I don't see how he lived through it.

Shortly after that the captain decided to get rid of all the rotten salt meat and fish we had left. This included beef (I still think it was horse), pork, cod and mackerel. Joe Kaplan was helping dump the meat when somebody handed him a chunk of pork and when he realized what it was he dropped it fast. He was upset and very angry.

We really liked Joe. He accidently dropped a spanner when he was on his way up a mast. It barely missed Archie, who said "You did that on purpose." Joe spent the next three days trying to apologize. Archie, of course, knew it was an accident but just wanted to get Joe going.

One of my most memorable meals was with Chips while we were being berthed by a tug in Cape Town. We traded some American cigarettes for black bread, eggs and butter. We took these to the galley and had fried fresh eggs, black bread (no weevils) and butter. It was delicious.

During the war South Africa did not have refined or white flour. Later, during our stay in Durban, some of us in the crew managed to get some white flour ashore from the *Tango* to American and Canadian families that had befriended us. They were most grateful and sifted out the weevils to make pastries and rolls.

In Cape Town I was fascinated by the Zulu rickshaws. They looked much like the Chinese rickshaws but the Zulu drivers handled them much differently. Instead of the short chop-chop steps of the Chinese, the Zulus balanced themselves on the traces and took long strides, it looked like they were running in slow motion. Archie and I had our pictures taken in one with him in the traces wearing a Zulu headdress and me on the seat.

While there I managed to make arrangements to attend a Royal Navy Morse code class with the possibility of continuing with them to improve my

Archie McPhee with headdress and Gene Luce (behind) clown with rickshaw and native. (From Luce collection.)

code speed. They were beyond my level but I was given a chance to both receive and send code. The instructor told me my receiving was weak but that I did have a good "fist", meaning sending a clear, easily readable signal. In the British and South African navies their sending keys are mounted at the edge of the desk with the knob protruding beyond the edge leaving the arm out in the open. I told the instructor that if the key was mounted in farther where I could rest my arm and just use my wrist, like mine on the *Tango*, I could probably do better. His tone was a little sarcastic when he said "If you think your way of placing the key is better than the Royal Navy's way, that's your prerogative". I told him it was not just my way but was the placement used by both the American Navy and the American Merchant Marine. He looked at me in almost shocked disbelief then turned and walked away. I should have gone back to the class but didn't.

At that time South Africa was bilingual and the white population was made of two divisions, the English heritage South Africans, known simply as South Africans and the Dutch heritage South Africans, known as Afrikaners. We were liked by the South Africans but not by the Afrikaners. We did learn not to ask South Africans on the street for directions as they would insist on taking us where we wanted to go rather than just giving us directions and then would want us to visit their homes. It was embarrassing at times.

We spent almost three months in Cape Town then made our way around and up the coast to Durban.

In Durban, after the cargo was unloaded we spent a long time at berth waiting for a new cargo and orders. During that period some of us spent a lot of time at the American Canadian Club drinking cokes, eating homemade doughnuts and playing ping-pong. Even with only one good eye Archie was the best ping-pong player at the Club. Archie also came up with a game of deck golf. We made our own wooden mallets and disks and laid out a course on the deck of the *Tango* somewhat like a croquet course. We played a lot of deck golf.

While there I pulled another stupid act. A couple of Afrikaner security guards were stationed at the dock gate 20 feet from the *Tango*. The guards confiscated two bottles of Scotch whiskey from two English sailors from another ship. After the sailors left, the guards had their backs to us talking intensely to a taxi driver we used often. I slipped across the wharf into the guard shack and picked up on of the bottles and returned to the ship without the guards seeing me.

When the guards returned to the shack they missed the bottle and at first thought each was playing a joke on the other, then they realized it was no joke. They came over to us and asked if we had seen anybody around the guard house. Of course we hadn't. The taxi driver also denied seeing anybody although we wondered afterward if he may have seen me. If they had caught me I'd been in real trouble.

There were a number of tearful farewells when we finally left Durban for Santos, Brazil, which was only natural since we had been there long enough for some to become involved in serious relationships. Just the same there wasn't one of us who wasn't glad to be on our way again.

It wasn't long before we hit our first big storm and from then on our forward cabins always had water in them. The darn ship would heel over one way and pick up water carrying a lot of it with it as it heeled the other way, sloshing the water through our alleyway and dumping it on the other side. Then it would continue to heel until it picked up more water on that side and reverse the process.

One thing about that storm that fascinated me was how much it reminded me of the dry gulches of western Nebraska where I used to go hunting. Except that one side of the trough was concave and the other convex. We couldn't see over the top of the waves and the trough extended from each side of the ship until it curved out of sight at either end. We would be lifted to the top of the next crest where we could see huge white caps from horizon to horizon until we would slide down into the next trough. I was always sorry we didn't have pictures of that.

With all that coal ballasting our ship we were reminded of kid's toys that were similarly ballasted with weights in their ball-shaped bottoms. They would have a clown or other figure on the top. When they were knocked over they would come right back up. That is the way the *Tango* acted except we were not certain she would come back every time she heeled way over.

Come back, the *Tango* always did, including back to Durban.

While in Durban the first time, Ira brought a dog aboard as a mascot. The dog had worms and we had Ira get some worm pills to take care of the problem. This led to another humorous anecdote during our second stay in Durban. In keeping with what Ira

213

considered the image of the Ancient Mariner he started chewing tobacco. He kept a gallon can of sand in his quarters to spit in which he neglected to dump as often as he should have. One day he came rushing up to Archie and me at the rail to tell us he was spitting up worms and took us back to his spittoon.

Archie and I realized maggots had formed on top of the sand but Ira really believed he was spitting up worms. Archie said, "The only thing to do is to take one of the dog's worm pills". Ira did and spent the night running to the head. Each time he did he would come back and pound on my door, he blamed me because I knew he was serious about the worms and Archie thought he was kidding.

Ira got even later by tossing a sand shark someone had caught through my porthole into my bunk while I was asleep. It was startling, to say the least, to wake up to find that slimy body in bed with me. I really didn't blame Ira, he was only evening the score.

After another long stay in Durban we were again underway with a ballast of smoldering coal to deliver the *Tango* to its new owners in Lourenco Marques, Portuguese East Africa. As we approached the mouth of the river leading up to Lourenco Marques, looking more like a steamer with the smoke coming out of our ventilators, I got the dubious opportunity to use my radio equipment.

The captain wanted me to radio in for a tug to take us up the river rather than trying to tack our way up but not to tell them we were on fire. I finally made contact and requested the tug. The station wanted to know what was wrong that required a tug to take us up the river. It took me considerable time to convince them there was nothing wrong but that we were a large sailing vessel and did not have room to tack up the river.

When I was finished, and with a chest inflated about six inches more than normal, I went to the captain and told him everything had been taken care of. The captain said, "Sparks, I've decided you had better call back and let them know we are on fire and to have a fire tug stand by". My chest quickly deflated. After convincing the port station nothing was wrong, I was quite embarrassed to call them back and tell them we did have one small problem, it was just that we are on fire."

(Note—Lourenco Marques, now called Maputo, is the capital and leading port of Mozambique, formerly Portuguese East Africa. It is located near the southern end of Mozambique and is close to South Africa.)

In this environment we weren't as welcome ashore as we were in South Africa. The first night ashore we celebrated with joy and some sadness that we had made our last trip on the *Tango* and would soon be on our way home. This celebration resulted in five of us ending up in jail, myself for five days.

After little more than a month most of the crew were paid off leaving only the captain, Archie, Joe, Ira and myself. Although the others remained another four months in Lourenco Marques, I was paid off a short time after the main body of the crew had left and put on a Liberty ship for home.

Within a couple of days of putting to sea I started getting sea sick, or so I thought, which I didn't understand after all I had been through on the *Tango*. I sure took a lot of good natured ribbing from the crew of the Liberty ship. It continued to get worse and three nights later I fell to the deck, still conscious but unable to move and my heart beating like a trip hammer. My cabin mate called the ship's medic and they got me into my bunk where I stayed.

I had gotten friendly with the bos'n who visited me regularly and we even kidded about him having to get a canvas shroud ready for me. I knew my illness started getting serious when the bos'n refused to kid that way anymore. Because I was so hot and had a high fever they took turns rubbing me down with ice bags.

Arriving in Aden, Africa, they sent me ashore in a sling and put me in a Royal Air Force hospital where I continued to grow worse. The doctors diagnosed my illness as typhoid, picked up in Lourenco Marques.

With typhoid you are not allowed solid foods and all I could have was fruit flavored water. I continued downhill, becoming delirious and the hospital was afraid I wasn't going to make it. They moved me from the main ward into what the other patients called 'the death room' where the most serious cases were taken and seldom were seen coming out.

I was too ill to know how things actually progressed but I gather I passed the crisis in that room and again was moved out into the main ward even though I was still somewhat delirious.

Eventually I came to with a clear head but my memory of the last two years was gone. The last I could remember was working in the harvest fields in Oregon and I had no idea how I ended up in Aden. I had lost so much weight I looked like a refugee from a concentration camp, I lacked about a quarter of an inch from being able to put one hand around my thigh bone. My hair was coming out by the handfuls and even the soles of my feet were peeling.

One of my first requests was for a small American flag to put on my bedside stand to show I was American, not British. The hospital contacted an American Air Force emergency airfield just outside Aden. The Americans brought me their company flag, trimmed in gold braid, and put it on the wall above my bed. Boy, was I proud. My only disappointment was the flag was on loan and I couldn't take it with me when I left Aden.

My ward was on the second floor of the hospital and I asked to be moved out onto the veranda where some of the patients had their beds and which overlooked the port facilities. When they did, it just so happened an Arab was going by below on a camel. I was so amazed, I had always wanted to travel and see things like this and here I was but still not remembering how I got here.

The day was July 25, 1944, just two days before my 21st birthday. The hospital baked a cake for me although I was allowed only a few bites since they were bringing me back to solid foods slowly.

Sister Kay Fyson, the nurse who gave me the most attention in the hospital, wrote my parents when things looked blackest, trying to prepare them for the possible worst. Unknown to the Sister, this was the first word they had of me since I had written to say I was being put on a ship for home, then simply disappeared. Because the letter had to go through censorship and the British postal system it took nearly three weeks to reach my parents. They were understandably shocked and also realized that by then the crises was passed but had no idea of the outcome.

By the time the letter reached them I had already recovered enough to dictate a letter to one of the American servicemen from the airfield, addressed to my parents. I was still very confused and the letter did not make a lot of sense but was mailed from the airfield. It reached my parents just three days after the nurse's and came as momentous relief to them.

After nearly three months and the complete return of my memory, I again found myself on a stretcher going aboard an English ship bound for Cairo, Egypt. I was leaving behind some good British friends and excellent treatment by the hospital staff. (After the war I was able to correspond with some of these friends back in England.) Since I went in on a stretcher and came out on a stretcher I never actually set foot in Aden.

In Cairo, I was moved from the ship to the 38th General American Army Hospital just outside Cairo. Here the army's priority was to get some meat back on my bones including, to the envy of other patients, giving me two ounces of liquor a day to improve my appetite.

When I became ambulatory again and circumstances allowed, I visited the American consul in Cairo in hopes that he could arrange passage for me back to the States. He asked me my name and I told him "Gene Luce". He said, "You are supposed to be dead. I was transferred from Aden and the day I left they told me you probably would not make it through the night. Congratulations on proving them wrong".

Before the American consul could arrange anything the army decided to fly me home. I had spent almost another three months in Egypt. One plane got me as far as Casablanca and the next to New York City with an early morning stop in Newfoundland.

In Egypt, just about everything we ate was prepared from powdered ingredients including powdered eggs and powdered milk. In Newfoundland I had my second most memorable meal of the past two and a half years. We were served fresh eggs, bacon and fresh whole milk. It was great!

We landed at LaGuardia air field. My only identification was the photostat of my birth certificate which I was told by the immigration officers that anybody could obtain. After some good natured ribbing from the two officers I was allowed through. If I hadn't come in on an Air Force plane, I think it would have been much more difficult.

I was able to get in touch with Captain Gundersen while in New York and we arranged to meet for dinner. First we stopped at a bar for a welcome home drink from the captain. The barman refused to serve me as he thought I was under 18, the legal limit. Actually I was 21 plus but looked young. Captain Gundersen was quite amused but was able to convince the bartender that I had been on his ship for over two years and had just returned from a long illness overseas. I enjoyed the drink.

In New York I met officials of the company that had owned the *Tango*. The best I was able to do was to get half the pay I was entitled to for the six months it took me to return to the states.

Before leaving New York I signed up for the draft then headed home to Nebraska to rest and recuperate. After being there two or three months I was interviewed by the local paper which ran a rather lengthy piece about the *Tango* and myself.

About the same time I received my A-1 draft notice. A few days later I appeared before the local draft board to ask for a deferment so I could return to New York to study for a radio operator's license. I wore my letterman's sweater that I had earned running in the mile race in high school. The first man asked me if I had graduated as yet and I said yes. The second man interrupted to ask if by any chance I was the boy whose picture had appeared in the paper with an article about my being aboard a sailing ship. I said I was. At their insistence, the next hour was spent relating sea stories until one of the men recalled why they and I were there. They granted me my deferment.

Back in New York I enrolled in an RCA radio school and also took a job as a page boy at NBC in Radio City.

Perry Como was appearing on the "Chesterfield Hour" at that time and would pitch pennies with the page boys, including me, before the program. He was liked by everyone and it was a real opportunity to meet him.

After obtaining my license I shipped out as 2nd Radio Officer on a Liberty ship bound for Marseille, France. After we had discharged our cargo and were pulling away from the dock, it was officially announced that the war in Europe was over. We sure missed a big celebration in Marseille.

After that trip I went to the West Coast and shipped in tankers plying in the Pacific until the Japanese surrendered.

*Gene Luce as a licensed radio officer following his **Tango** experience.*

Again going back to Nebraska I attended a junior college for a year and a half before returning to the sea. On a short run to Cuba, I met a passenger Eleanor Dietlin from Massachusetts. After less than a two week whirlwind courtship and seven months corresponding while I was at sea we were married April 28, 1951. After nearly forty years of marriage I consider myself a very lucky man.

Luce made only one more trip as a radio officer after his marriage, then "swallowed the anchor" and came ashore for good to settle down as a family man. He intended to return to Scottsbluff to work in the sugar factory. Instead he side-slipped to Baton Rouge, La., to complete some courses related to sugar manufacture at Louisiana State University.

He graduated with a degree in chemical engineering and went to work as an engineer for a sugar factory at Reserve, La. During the ensuing 32 years he was an engineer or plant manager in syrup, fruit punch and other food processing plants at New Orleans, La.; Burlington, Vt.; Atlanta, Ga.; Winston-Salem, N.C.; and Seagrove, N.C., much of the time for R. J. Reynolds Food Division.

He retired at age 65 on 38 acres of woodland near Seagrove where he loves working in the garden and landscaping around home. Two of Gene's and Eleanor's three daughters are married and are raising six grandchildren.

APPENDIX

Appendix A

Minutes of Crew Meetings

Notes kept by Archie McPhee of meetings by the union crew during the voyage from St. Helens to South Africa.

Special Meeting, May 22, 1942

Called to order at 6 p.m.

Motion by Moller, seconded by Varellas, to hold a regular meeting every Friday. Carried.

Motion by Kaplan, seconded by McPhee, for crew to live up to union working rules. Carried. (Crew are members of the Sailors Union of the Pacific.)

Motion by Moller that all dirty work to be performed on watch to be split up as evenly as possible. Seconded. Carried.

Motion made and seconded to conduct ourselves as union men and bring all beefs pertaining to union up at our meetings. Carried.

Meeting adjourned at 7 p.m., to be continued tomorrow.

Regular Meeting, May 29

Called at 6 p.m. Minutes of previous meeting read.

New business: Discussion on port holes and leakage of overhead. Motion by St. Clair that each watch take care of its port holes. Second, carried.

Leak at anchor chains; to be pulled in so we can make hawsepipes watertight.

On grub: Check on canned meats, ask for more pastries, salmon on the menu, toaster to be left out, to use more fresh lunch meat before we go into canned stuff. No evident beefs to be held over on grub.

Good and welfare—conserve on coal. List of slop chest prices, mate is getting it.

Motion on former action that we hold meetings once a week. Made by Jones, seconded and carried.

Motion by Varellas, seconded, meetings to be called as necessary. Carried. Adjourned at 6:30 p.m.

Meeting, June 6

Called to order at 6 p.m. Angelo nominated chairman and elected by acclamation. Secretary, McPhee. Minutes of last meeting read and accepted.

On grub, no toaster as yet, no lunch several nights.

New business: Motion by Burke to elect a new delegate. Delegate had resigned. Nominations—Kaplan and Varellas. Kaplan elected.

Motion by Moller: Members to correct and train those not as familiar with sailing ships and those shown to accept graciously. Carried.

(Scratched, but discussed: Cook and messboy asked into the meeting. Proposition put to cook and messboy for them to split difference in wages between them and messboy to cook, the cook to continue baking, the rest of the work to be split between them. They are to offer their decision tomorrow.)

Moved and seconded to adjourn at 7 p.m.

Meeting, June 12

Meeting called at 6 p.m. Jones elected chairman by acclamation. Minutes of last meeting read and accepted.

New business: Motion by Kaplan to bar Cheney from meetings. Seconded by Varellas. Carried. Delegate instructed to tell Cheney that he has been barred from the meetings; also that the crew looks down on him for his lack of respect towards the union.

List of demands to be presented to the captain:
1. Two lanterns for the messroom.
2. Lifeline along each side of the crew quarters.

3. Steps and stanchions on port side to messroom.
4. Portholes in toilets and washroom to be made seaworthy.
5. Proper facilities for washroom.
6. Doors to be fitted properly.
7. Adequate lighting under the foc'sle head.

List approved and delegate instructed to present the list to the captain at his earliest opportunity.

Motion by Kaplan: Committee of three men to check stores. Seconded. Nominations: Jones, Varellas, Moller, Kaplan. Moller declined in favor of Kaplan. Others accepted and passed by membership.

Good and welfare: Noticed by membership there is a lot more cooperation and the older fellows have been instructing those less versed in sailing ship work. Lively discussion held by all.

Adjourned at 6:30.

Meeting, Saturday, August 8

Meeting called at 12:30 p.m. Varellas elected chairman. Minutes of previous meeting read.

Motion by Kaplan to rescind former action of barring Ira Cheney from meetings. Seconded and carried, and Cheney is to be given another chance to attend meetings, but in event he reveals any of the proceedings of our union meetings he will be barred from future meetings and also from member-ship into the Sailors Union of the Pacific. Minutes of last meeting accepted.

New business: None.

Good and welfare: List of demands:
1. Seaworthy lifeboats to be provided before ship
   sails (from Cape Town).
2. Insulate forward bulkhead of boiler room against
   fire and fumes.
3. All toilets on ship to be overhauled and made
   more efficient.
4. Necessary repairs to all foc'sle doors.

5. Scuppers in toilets, foc'sle, bathroom, and under foc'sle head.
6. All portholes to be made seaworthy.
7. Hospital to be used only as sick bay and for medicine chest, and to be made ready for immediate occupation.
8. A more complete slop chest on the return voyage.
9. Scuppers in galley and messroom.
10. All quarters to be painted.
11. All broken and rusted rails to be renewed.
12. Bunk shelves in all bunks.
13. Bunk lamps in all bunks.
14. Small kerosene stove to make coffee in warm weather.
15. Three dozen wicks for heaters.
16. One-half dozen heaters.
17. One dozen kerosene lanterns.
18. Two dozen galvanized buckets.
19. Repair overhead, etc. of the O.S. room.
20. Salt water soap. Also demand penalty of 2 hours weekly for not furnishing salt water soap from Portland to Africa.
21. Draw in American money.
22. Clean and cement domestic tanks.
23. Messboy and steward to be signed immediately on arrival.
24. Coal stove under foc'sle head.
25. Washing machine.
26. Six life preservers in box on poop.
27. Life raft for eight seamen on for'd hatch.
28. Caulk beams and timbers of quarters against leakage.
29. Wooden eaves for doors and portholes for'd.

Motion made and carried to adjourn at 1:46.

To Capt. Gundersen: August 17, 1942, SV *Tango*

We, the crew of this vessel, present to you these demands because we deem them necessary to safeguard our lives and health.

1. A metal cap for the wheel, to protect the life of the helmsman.
2. Both store rooms to be cleaned out and the food stores to be thoroughly examined; those stores unfit for use to be removed from the ship.

With anticipation of your cooperation.

The Crew.

Meeting August 28 (In Cape Town)

Meeting called at 1:30. Burke elected chairman. Minutes of previous meeting read and accepted.

New business: Motion by Kaplan to ask for payoff because of unseaworthiness of ship. Amendment to motion by Moller—withdrawn. Motion by Moller: That we draw up a petition asking for a mandatory survey of this ship and a decision as to whether this ship was seaworthy before she sailed. In case of a favorable decision, we go on record to be paid off as prescribed by law. Seconded by Sampson, carried.

Motion by Kaplan, seconded by Green: For three copies of petition to be drawn up. Motion carried.

Motion by Sampson, seconded by Green, that we postpone action on note of 28/8/42 regarding demands. Motion carried. (Note follows).

Adjourned at 2:30.

Aug. 28, 1942. Cape Town

We, the undersigned members of the SV *Tango*, do hereby certify that on July 2nd, at about 3 a.m. while riding a bad storm, a sea was shipped breaking both lifeboats free of their lashings. A. Bitte, being on lookout at the time, notified the Captain and the Chief Mate, but no attempt was made to save the lifeboats or their equipment. A. Varellas was at the wheel at the time. He also notified the Mate about the boats, and again nothing was done about trying to save the lifeboats and their equipment. Varellas then asked the Mate to get someone else at the wheel and he himself would try to save whatever he could of the boats, whereupon the Chief Mate remarked that there was absolutely nothing that could be done about the boats in a storm as bad as that. Yet, when the following watch came on at 4 a.m. the Chief Mate ordered the second mate to get the boats secured although the storm had not moderated. This was done immediately, saving what was left of the boats and their equipment.

Jas. E. Burke, 2nd Mate   Fred Bitte, Carpenter
Angelo Varellas, A.B.

Meeting Sept. 1

Meeting called to order at 4 p.m. Burke elected chairman. Minutes of previous meeting read and accepted.

New business: Delegate's report on results of our petition.

Motion by Sampson: To sit tight and have the steward see the consul. Withdrawn. Amendment by Moller to wait and see what action we get on the steward's next order. Carried.

Motion by Moller to find out what is holding up the ship. The delegation of three to be J. Kaplan, delegate; J. Burke, bos'n; and H. Jones, A.B. Carried. Adjourned at 4:30 p.m.

Business Meeting Sept. 18

Meeting called at 12:30 p.m. Kaplan elected chairman by acclamation. Minutes of previous meeting read and accepted.

New business: Motion by Jones for each member to make out his statement on the seaworthiness of the ship and give it to the delegate as soon as possible. Carried.

Motion by Burke to make up a list of unseaworthy items concerning the ship for the members to use in making out their statements. Carried.

Motion by St. Clair for Moller to invite the mate to our meeting. Carried.

Mate refused to attend meeting and says he has no more to say about the boats than what he has already said.

228

Good and welfare:
1. Dent in inboard side of starboard boat having been there the entire trip.
2. Mate's statement about his knowledge of holes having been there the entire trip.
3. Carpenter's report on rusty condition of boats when he repaired them.
4. Report on having found holes in boats after storm.
5. Regarding bilge pumps.
6. Turnbuckles on steering wheel.
7. No steering oar in either boat and no rudder in the port boat at all.

(No mention of adjournment.)

Meeting Nov. 26

Meeting called to order at 1 p.m. Burke elected chairman. Minutes of previous meeting read and accepted.

New business: None.

Unfinished business: None.

Delegate's report, accepted.

Good and welfare: Moved and accepted to take present list of demands for acceptance or rejection. Carried.

Motion by Kaplan for two men, Sampson and Jones, to accompany him to the Captain when he presents him with the demands. Carried.

List of Demands
1. Clean and cement domestic tanks and move them below deck.
2. Practical ice box.
3. Hospital to be for original purpose.
4. Store room to be made sanitary for food and safe for a human to enter.
5. Uniform shelves for all bunks.
6. All toilets to be checked and repaired.
7. Additional scuppers for washroom and under foc'sle head.
8. Brackets for cover of hawsepipe to be repaired.

9. One dozen porthole crystals and rings. One ring wrench.
10. Two dozen lamp wicks. Two dozen of type of lamp chimneys.
11. Six lanterns, one dozen galvanized buckets, salt water soap.
12. Fifteen army cots.
13. Keys for crew's quarters.
14. Thwartship, spare sailors' foc'sle to be made into reading room and coal stove to be installed in it to heat it and both watch foc'sles.
15. Shelter for helmsman.
16. Repair O.S. quarters.
17. Bunker hatch aft for stowing coal.
18. Rattle down the rigging.
19. Fully stock slop chest.
20. Emergency alarm to be installed throughout ship.
21. Foc'sle deck to be painted for waterproofing.
22. Lifeboat awning, rail and dodgers for boats.
23. Fix and repair lifeboat davits.
24. Doors to be made watertight. All quarters to be painted.
25. Electric capstan on poop for raising sails and mooring.
26. Two life rafts, one for'd and one aft.
27. One dozen life preservers to be placed for emergency.
28. Scuppers for foc'sle, galley and messroom.
29. Mushroom ventilation for messroom and amidship quarters.
30. Check and restock medicine chest.
31. Wooden eaves over all portholes and doors.
32. Skylights in sailors' foc'sle for emergency escape.
33. Larger sink in place of present one in galley and a concealed sink.

34. Skylight in front of boilers in engine room for emergency escape.
35. Gates for washports.
36. That the $25,000 wage guarantee is on deposit before we sail, as per agreement.
37. Replace centrifugal pump on diesel engine with plunger or rotary pump.
38. Install hand standby pumps for sea water lines to sanitary tanks, also for diesel oil to burners.
39. New carburetor and magnets to Delco plant for emergency.
40. Two extra bulbs for battery charger.
41. Two foamite fire extinguishers for engine room.
42. Fifty-pound anvil, small forge, and forge tools.

Special Meeting Nov. 27

Meeting called to order at 6 p.m. Kaplan elected chairman by acclamation. Order of meeting—revision of demands.

Motion by Sampson, seconded by Burke, to turn in revised list of demands to Captain and keep old list for reference on returning to the States. Accepted.

Motion by Burke: Messboy to fulfill his duties or to be locked up, his pay stopped, and to be brought up before the American consul on charges. Dropped.

Revised List
1. That the $25,000 wage guarantee is to be on deposit in escrow before we sail, as per our agreement.
2. Clean and cement domestic tanks and move them below deck for safety.
3. Practical ice box.
4. Storeroom to be made sanitary for food and safe for human being to enter.
5. Brackets for cover of hawsepipe to be repaired.
6. Repair O.S. quarters.
7. Emergency alarm to be installed throughout ship.
8. Foc'sle deck heads to be painted.

9. Lifeboat awning, dodgers and rails for boats.
10. Repair lifeboat davits.
11. Doors to be made watertight and quarters to be painted out.
12. Two life rafts, one for'd, one aft.
13. One dozen life preservers to be placed aft for emergency.
14. Check and restock medicine chest and slop chest.
15. Skylight in sailors' foc'sle and engine room for emergency escapes.
16. Gates for wash ports.

Special Meeting Dec. 8

Meeting called to order at 12:30. Jones made chairman by acclamation. Subject: Crew's draw.

Motion by Burke that the two men having Wednesday off, Jones and McPhee, go to the American consul and tell him that we demand full draw, which consists of half our wages.

If we do not get the draw by Thursday night, we shall walk off the ship Friday morning and attach it for enough to pay off the entire crew, as prescribed by law. Seconded and passed.

Meeting adjourned at 1:00 p.m.

Special Meeting, Dec. 24, 1942

Meeting called to order at 11 a.m. Kaplan acting chairman. Subject: Election of bos'n. Hans Moller, the only nominee, received all the votes of the five S.U.P. book members present.

Good and welfare: Took up a collection for the members of the *Commodore*, who are stranded S.U.P. men, so they could have a little pocket money for Christmas.

List of donors: C. Hammer, J. Kaplan, H. Moller, I. Cheney, O. Lindbergh, J. Sampson, R. Cross, A. McPhee, G. Luce, S. Bowyer—each 10 shillings; R. Berlin, 20 shillings.

Appendix B

Transition
From Sail to Steam to Motor
and Back to Sail

Ever since man began his efforts to master the waters he has made slow but sure progress. His first ship may have been a log which he paddled, followed by a group of logs lashed together to form a raft. Next may have been canoes made of reeds, or logs hollowed out, or skins of animals or bark fastened together over crude frameworks, or even clay pots bundled together. Is that where the term "vessel" originated?

Then, some 5,000 years ago, an enterprising body in Egypt was believed to have invented a sail for his canoe and started a new fad, letting the wind push his craft. This was followed by boats made of wooden planks with sails stretched on one or two wooden masts, with rudders and ropes to guide the sails.

Thus the commercial sailing ship came into being for carrying men and their trade goods across big waters such as the Mediterranean, and eventually over oceans.

Vessels propelled by wind or paddles continued to be the mode for centuries, until 1783, when a French nobleman, the Marquis Claude de Jouffroy d'Abbans, launched a small steam-propelled boat with side paddle wheels in the Saone River, near Lyons, France. It was the first steamboat but failed to run after 15 minutes.

Men continued to tinker and experiment with steam-powered craft and in 1787 the first workable steamboat made its appearance. It was built by Robert Fitch, an American engineer, for passenger service on the Delaware River. It was 60 feet long and was propelled by six paddles on each side.

The first successful steamboat was the *Clermont*, designed and built by another American, Robert Fulton, in 1807 for service on the Hudson River between New York and Albany. It had a small English-built engine with a single small cylinder and it received its steam from a wood-fired boiler. Long and lean, the boat was 142 feet by 14 feet, with paddle wheels 15 feet in diameter and four feet wide.

The *Clermont* made trips between New York and Albany, a distance of 150 miles, in 52 hours, an average speed of about three miles an hour. It was named for the home of Robert R. Livingston, who helped Fulton in construction of the vessel and previously helped draw up the Declaration of Independence.

Two years later, another American, John Stephens, built the steamboat *Phoenix*, which made the first ocean voyage—from New York to Philadelphia.

Meanwhile, British builders were developing iron ships, stronger and safer than vessels of wood. The first iron steamship was the *Aaron Manby*, launched in 1821 in England.

The first steamship to cross the Atlantic Ocean was the wooden American ship *Savannah*, which sailed and steamed from Savannah, Georgia, to England in 1819. It had masts and sails which were used most of the time. The steam engine was used only 85 hours in the 29-day passage.

In 1838, the British steamship *Sirius* crossed the Atlantic as the first vessel to use steam power only—no sails.

The first iron steamship built for regular Trans-Atlantic service was the 236-foot *Great Western*, launched in England in 1838. It had masts and sails as well as the steam engine.

Twenty years later, the mammoth *Great Eastern*, 692 feet long, was launched in England to carry 4,000 passengers on the Atlantic, but it failed financially. It finally was put to work as a cable ship to lay the first Trans-Atlantic telegraph cable between New York and England. It also had masts and sails. It was scrapped in 1888.

Screw propellers were invented and patented in 1836 by Francis Pettit Smith, an Englishman, and by John Ericsson, a Swede. Propellers proved to be more efficient than side paddle wheels, which lifted out of the water when a ship rolled in heavy seas. The steamship *Great Britain*, 322 feet long, was the first propeller ship to cross the Atlantic Ocean.

While steamships were assuming a place in the ocean transportation world, sailing vessels also were getting larger and more efficient. The first full-rigged vessels were developed for service in the Mediterranean about 1450, and various types of sails and rig configurations came along in due time.

The largest of all sailing vessels was the *France II*, a 5-masted bark built in France in 1911, of 5,633 gross tons. Other leading big vessels were the *R. C. Rickmers*, German 5-masted bark, built in 1906, 5,548 gross tons; *Thomas W. Lawson*, 7-masted American schooner, built in 1902, 5,081 gross tons; *Preussen*, German 5-masted ship built in 1902, 5,081 gross tons. The *France II* and *R. C. Rickmers* were equipped with auxiliary steam engines and therefore were not exclusively sailing vessels. The American schooner *Thomas W. Lawson* could be considered largest of all true sailing vessels.

France II carried 65,000 square feet of sail, had 30 miles of running rigging, and her main truck towered 200 feet above the waterline. She was employed in transporting coal from England to New Caledonia, returning via Cape Horn with nickel ore. She was wrecked on the coast of New Caledonia in 1922.

Probably the most important last stand for sailing cargo ships was the coal and nitrate trade between Europe and the West Coast of South America in which *Hans* and scores of other vessels under the flags of Germany, England and France participated during the late 1800s and early 1900s, before the

Panama Canal shortened the distances and steamships took over.

New types of power were developed during the same late 1800s and early 1900s. First came the steam turbine, more powerful and efficient than the steam engine. It was invented in the late 1890s by Charles A. Parsons, an English engineer. Steam turbines soon were being installed in luxury liners on the Atlantic and they still are popular with shipbuilders and owners.

Next came the oil-burning diesel engine, developed by a German engineer, Rudolph Diesel, in the early 1900s. The first motorships with diesel engines came out about 1910 and diesel engines now are more widely used than other types of power for large ships. Oil replaced coal as fuel.

Yet another type of sea-going energy has been developed in more recent years—nuclear power. The first nuclear-powered merchant ship was launched in 1959 and given the name of a famed forerunner, *Savannah*. It operated in the American merchant service for 12 years, but was retired in 1971 as impractical for commercial service because of high building and operating costs. Nuclear power, however, propels various American naval vessels and submarines.

Steam and motor-driven ships spelled the death knell for large commercial sailing vessels and few, if any, exist today. Several nations have tall sailing training ships in their navies and sailing is more popular than ever for small cruising and racing craft, competing in popularity with motor-driven sports boats.

However, the winds continue to blow and gradually rising cost of petrofuels have prompted enterprising mariners to experiment with new uses for sails. Freighters have been fitted with sails designed to make use of ocean winds as auxiliary to steam and diesel power.

Capt. Jacques Costeau, the French oceanographer, has outfitted his 103-foot *Alcyone* with wind-driven funnels which turn propellers through a system of gears and shafts and has displayed it widely.

More recently, a Miami, Florida, based tourist company, Wind Star Sail Cruises, Ltd., commissioned a French shipyard to build four 440-foot cruise ships propelled in part by wind power. The first fleet member, *Wind Star*, went into service in the Caribbean, carrying 150 passengers in deluxe cabins. The second, *Wind Song*, was placed in service operating seven-day voyages out of Tahiti. Two more sister ships were reported completed and in service by 1990.

These 5,350-ton vessels have four masts with six triangular self-furling, computer-controlled sails with 21,700 square feet of surface area. Auxiliary power is provided by diesel-electric engines.

More recently a 617-foot cruise ship with computer controlled sails, the *Club Med II*, has gone into service in the Caribbean and Mediterranean areas. It has five masts.

So, as long as the winds blow, sailing ships may again become popular ocean transport vehicles.

Appendix C

Shipbuilding in World War I

To provide ship tonnage for the Allies as well as for its own domestic purposes, the United States launched more than 2,000 vessels of 1,000 gross tons or larger during World War I.

The Department of Commerce's *Merchant Vessels of the United States*, 1933 edition, listed 1,878 steam, gas, or motor-driven steel-hulled vessels of more than 1,000 gross tons built in U.S. shipyards during the war period, 1914-1919, inclusive.

During the same period, 186 sailing vessels—schooners, barkentines and barks—of more than 1,000 gross tons were launched. Many of these hulls were wooden.

Of the steel vessels, 729 were of more than 5,000 gross tons. The largest were the *Andrea Luckenbach* and *Lewis Luckenbach*, each of 10,800 gross tons, built at Quincy, Mass.; and the tankers *Achilles* and *Ulysses*, each of 11,000 gross tons, built at Newport News, Va.

During the post-war years, 1920-1921, many additional vessels of both steel and wood construction were launched by shipyards completing wartime contracts and for private owners.

Many of the new ships were turned over to friendly foreign nations.

Pacific Coast shipyards produced 315 steel vessels and 235 wooden ones during the war period. Many of the wooden vessels intended for steam or diesel power were finished as sailing schooners for coastwise and Pacific Ocean operation. Wooden hulls were expendable and were abandoned or burned when they became uneconomical.

Appendix D

The *Moshulu*, ex-*Kurt*

The S.V. *Moshulu, Tango*'s sister, was another great ship, built at Glasgow as the *Kurt*, and was renamed *Moshulu* in 1917. She was launched April 20, 1904, a few weeks after the *Hans*. She was large, fast and efficient during the years she was owned and operated by G. J. H. Siemers & Co. of Hamburg, and made 10½ round trips between Europe and Chile, and four side trips to Australia to bring coal to South American copper smelters. She carried more than 120,000 long tons of fuel and nitrate.

When World War I broke out, *Kurt* was at Santa Rosalia, Baja California, where she had just completed discharging a cargo of coke, but she sailed immediately for the Columbia River to load grain under charter. She successfully eluded Canadian warships along the Pacific Coast and arrived at Astoria, Oregon, September 11, 1914. She had a passenger, Senor Romano, the governor of Baja California, who was fleeing for his life from revolutionaries.

Kurt was at Astoria for two years and seven months. During the annual Astoria Regatta in September 1915, Captain Wilhelm Tonissen graciously allowed his ship to be used as a grandstand for the racing events.

When the United States entered the war against Germany, April 6, 1917, the U.S. government seized the *Kurt* and transferred Captain Tonissen and his remaining crew to a Georgia prison camp. The ship was towed to Portland and prepared for service under the direction of the United States Shipping Board. Her name was changed to *Dreadnaught* and with an American crew she sailed to San Francisco to load for the Far East.

While in the Bay area, the vessel's name was again changed, this time to *Moshulu*, the name she still carries. This name was assigned by Mrs. Woodrow Wilson, wife of the American President, who assigned Indian names to other German vessels taken over by the United States. *Moshulu* was said to be an Indian term meaning "fearless" and came from a Choctaw chief who gained some fame for winning battles with the Creeks in Mississippi in 1812.

During the next two years the *Moshulu* made three voyages between San Francisco and Australia, calling also in Hong Kong and the Philippines.

The Shipping Board sold the vessel in 1921 to the Charles Nelson Co., of San Francisco, for $29,505. Nelson was engaged in hauling lumber and sent the *Moshulu* on five round trips to the Far East, one trip around the world, and two coastwise voyages before the freight market played out. The ship was laid up at Oakland, California, for four years. In 1927 she made one voyage to Australia and upon return was laid up in Seattle for four years.

Captain Gustaf Erikson, of Mariehamn, Finland, became interested in the big ship for use in his wheat service from southern Australia to the British Isles and bought her from Nelson for $12,000 on March 14, 1935. Towed to Esquimalt, British Columbia, the vessel was drydocked, repaired, and acquired some sails from the former Alaska Packers bark *Star of England.*

Moshulu made four voyages with grain from Port Lincoln and Port Victoria, Australia, to England in 1936, 1937, 1938, and 1939, and one voyage from England to Buenos Aires and return with grain. The four grain race voyages took the ship around the world, south from Europe through the Atlantic Ocean to Cape of Good Hope, east to Australia, thence on across the Pacific Ocean to Cape Horn and north to the British Isles, some 30,000 nautical miles.

Moshulu, Tango's sister ship, at Penn's Landing, Philadelphia, was a popular floating restaurant and maritime museum, 1976 to 1989. (Photo by Capt. Gene Harrower, Portland, Ore.)

One of the *Moshulu*'s apprentices was J. Ferrell Colton, then 23, who later wrote about his experience in his books. Like eight other young men in the crew, he earned the princely sum of 100 Finnish marks per month.

An apprentice in the *Moshulu* during the last grain race was Erik Newby, an 18-year-old English boy who later wrote an interesting account of the voyage in his book, *The Last Grain Race*, published first by Martin Secker & Warburg, Ltd., in 1956, and later in 1981 by Granada Publishing Ltd., London.

Moshulu won the last race over 13 other big windjammers, all but two of which were four-masted barks. She carried a crew of 28, and in that race made her 25th passage around the Horn.

When the *Moshulu* returned to the Baltic in 1942, she was appropriated by the German military and rigged-down to a barge for the storage of grain. Her masts and rigging were destroyed by bombing during the war. While being towed between ports in Sweden and Norway, she was aground once and refloated, and at another time capsized in a storm, later to be raised and repaired.

In 1948 the hulk was sold to a Miss Gisken Jacobsen for two million Finnish marks (about $20,000 U.S.), and soon after was again sold, this time to Trygve Sommerfelt, a Norwegian, for use in grain storage at Stockholm, Sweden. Four years later she was purchased by a German firm to be rebuilt into a cargo and training ship, a project never completed.

In 1968 an American company, Specialty Restaurants Corporation, purchased the hull and towed it to Amsterdam, Holland, where it was refitted with new steel masts and bowsprit. She was towed across the Atlantic to New York by the German tug *Fair Play X*, arriving at Staten Island September 29, 1972.

Later she was moved to Philadelphia where she was converted into a floating restaurant and maritime museum at

Penn's Landing, at a cost reported to be $2 million. She was a popular attraction there from 1976 until June 1989, when a fire broke out in the restaurant, driving 200 diners into the street.

She lay idle until May 1990, when tugboats moved her across the Delaware River to Camden to await restoration into a seagoing sailing vessel at an estimated cost of $6 million.

However, later word on the *Moshulu*'s future was contained in this note in the May, 1991, issue of *Sea History Gazette*, published by the National Maritime History Society, Croton-on-Hudson, N.Y.:

> "Growing concern over the fate of the bark *Moshulu*, the largest square-rigger afloat, has prompted many to call on ship preservationists to make efforts to save the ship. (She) is languishing in Camden, Philadelphia (sic), being slowly stripped of everything of value aboard. Her end may be as a shell beached in Miami and established as a restaurant by Japanese interests if action isn't taken soon. Plans to have the *Moshulu* restored as a conference center at Fisherman's wharf in San Francisco have not materialized."

The last of her generation, *Moshulu* had ten owners and sailed under five flags.

It would be a shame for her to go the way of the *Tango*.

Appendix E

Some Nautical Terms Applicable to Sailing Vessels

Abaft—to the rear, after part of ship.

Aft—toward the stern.

Amidships—middle part of the ship, between bow and stern.

Ballast—heavy material carried in holds to keep vessel stable, not easily overturned.

Bark, Barque—three or more-masted vessel with square sails on all masts except after mast, which has fore-and-aft sails.

Barkentine, Barquentine—three or more-masted vessel with square sails on foremast and fore-and-aft sails on other masts.

Beam—width of ship at widest point.

Below—under the main deck, a lower level.

Binnacle—stand that holds the compass.

Block—frame in which one or more pulleys are mounted, used for lifting heavy objects.

Bollard—iron or wooden post on deck of ship or on dock for fastening hawsers.

Bow—forward portion of ship.

Bowsprit—spar or boom extending beyond bow, used for extending small sails.

Bridge—elevated deck from which ship is steered.

Brig—prison or guardhouse. Also, a two-masted square-rigged vessel.

Bulkhead—partition dividing ship into compartments.

Bulwarks—walls around decks to protect people, cargo and gear from falling out, and to keep out water in rough seas.

Capsize—to upset or overturn.

Claw—end of hoist with pronged grasp.

Cleat—wood or metal piece used to fasten ropes.

Clew—corner of a sail from which it is controlled.

Companionway—stairs from one deck to another.

Cringle—small loop or ring in edge of sail to put rope through.

Donkey—small steam engine used to assist in raising sails or handling cargo.

Donkeyman—crew member who operates donkey engine.

Draft—depth of ship below waterline.

Forecastle (foc'sle)—raised deck at bow, for sailors' quarters, supplies and machinery.

Forward—toward front end of ship.

Freeboard—side of ship between waterline and main deck.

Full-rigged ship—vessel with three or more masts all with square sails.

Halyard—rope or tackle for hoisting sails, yards, flags.

Hatch, hatchway—opening in deck to lower cargo into hold.

Hatch cover—cover over hatch opening.

Hawse hole, hawse pipe—hole in bow for putting hawser or cable through.

Hawser—large, heavy rope used for towing or securing ship.

Helm—ship's steering wheel.

Helmsman—crew member manning steering wheel.

Hold—space below deck where cargo is stowed.

Hove-to—stopped dead in water.

Jib—triangular sail extended from jib boom or bowsprit.

Jib boom—spar continuing from bowsprit.

Jibe—to shift sails from side to side when wind is abaft; motion of sail or boom when jibing.

Keel—external structure along middle of bottom.

Keelson—internal beam on floor timbers over the keel.

Lazy jack—line from above used to keep sail from whipping around.

Leech—edge of sail not fastened to rope or spar.

Lee side—side of ship away from or sheltered from wind.

Leeward—side away from the wind.

Martingale—short, perpendicular spar under bowsprit or a stay from such a spar to jib boom.

Mast—perpendicular timber or metal standard on deck to support sails.

Masthead—top of ship's mast. To send a man to top of mast for punishment.

Moor—to tie ship to dock or buoy, or to another ship with ropes, cables, or chains; or to anchor ship.

Poop—raised deck at stern. A wave breaking over deck or stern.

Port—left side of ship, also called larboard. A harbor or city where ships load and discharge cargo.

Quarter—sections on each side near stern of ship. Port quarter is left side; starboard quarter is on right side.

Quarters—lodgings for officers or crew.

Reef—fold in sail to reduce size. Sail may be reefed in extremely heavy winds.

Rigger—person who installs and fits rigging.

Rigging—ropes and equipment used to support and work sails.

Schooner—sailing vessel with two or more masts and fore-and-aft sails.

Shipping Board splice—a tie of two lines together by means of two or three clamps.

Shrouds—rope or wire supports at side of mast.

Spar—pole or timber used for masts, yards, booms.

Square rigger—sailing vessel with principal square sails across the masts.

Square sail—four-sided sail carried on a horizontal yard athwart the ship.

Stanchion—upright bar or beam to support bulwarks or other structures.

Starboard—right side when facing forward.

Stays—rope or wire used to support mast in fore or aft position.

Stem—timber or metal which unites sides at foremost part of bow of ship.

Superstructure—structure built above main deck.

Tack—change in direction. Also, line to lower leading corner of fore-and-aft sail.

Tackle—ropes and rigging of ship.

Topping lift—tackle for hoisting outer end of boom or yard.

Truck—circular or square piece of wood at top of mast.

Vessel—any large boat or ship for carrying cargo or passengers.

Watch—duty time for crew members working alternate periods, varying from two, four, or six to eight hours.

Windjammer—sailing vessel, especially square-rigged. Crew member of a sailing vessel.

Windlass—machine for lifting or pulling, as for raising an anchor.

Windward side—side exposed to the wind, the weather side.

Wing and wing—sails fully extended on each side.

Yard—spar fitted crosswise on mast to which sail is secured.

Index

249

H

Hahn, Bill 55
Halliburton, Richard 202
Hamburg, Germany 13, 18
Hamilton, Wm. & Co. 14, 17
Hammer, Chuck 54
Hancock, Jack 160
HANS, bark 10, 13, 20 - 21,
    31, 57, 198
Harrower, Capt. Eugene 12
Heydenrich, C. 185, 187
Holt, Peter L. 50, 67, 157, 185
Horn (Hoorn) Island 106, 109
Hotel Central Moderno 22 - 23
Huerta, Victoriano 22
Huycke, Capt. Harold D. 11, 18

I

IDZUMA, cruiser 24
Iguassu Falls 116
ILLIRIA, ship 114
INFLEXIBLE, battleship 112
INVERUGLAS, ship 47
INVINCIBLE, battleship 112
Iquique, Chile 17

J

JIM BUTLER, steamship 23,
    26
JOHANNA SMITH, barge 36
Johannesburg, South Africa
    152
Jones, Howard 54, 146

K

Kaasa, Arne 189
Kaasinen, Arne 188
Kaplan, Joe 54, 74, 77, 87,
    140, 146, 150, 157 - 158, 187,
    192, 194, 203, 208
KENILWORTH, ship 36, 39

Kimberly 152
KNAPPTON, tugboat 57, 62
Kuelsen, Capt. Jurgen F. 17, 20
KURT, bark 14, 18, 28, 39

L

LaGuardia air field 219
La Paz, Mexico 19
LADY WASHINGTON, ship
    109
Lawyer, Roy 143
LEIPSIG, cruiser 24
LeMaire, Issac 108
LeMaire, Strait of 108
LeMon, Charles 55
Lindberg, Ollie 158, 163, 168,
    176, 188, 192
Lisbon, Portugal 197
Lobito, Angola 197
Long Beach, California 11, 36,
    140
Los Angeles Shipbuilding &
    Drydock Corp. 41
Los Angeles, California 26
Louisiana State University 222
Lourenco Marques 187, 190,
    194, 197, 214
Luce, Gene 55, 68, 127, 187,
    194, 200

M

Maddison, John 168
Magallanes, Chile 112
Magellan, Ferdinand 106
Magellan, Strait of 107 - 109,
    111 - 112
Maputo 215
MARIE, schooner 41
Marine Cooks and Stewards
    Assn. 143
Mariners Museum 11
Marseille, France 220

Y

Archie McPhee

Archibald D. McPhee, the able-bodied seaman whose "log" of the *Tango*'s wartime voyage prompted this report, was born in Minnesota and grew up in Portland, Oregon. He went to sea on steamships in 1939. When he heard that a large sailing ship was loading at St. Helens he left his job as a shipyard rigger to volunteer for a place in the crew. Before sailing, he married his sweetheart, Ferne. She was waiting when he returned more than two years later. He came ashore, engaged in various businesses and retired in 1975. Archie and Ferne raised six daughters. He died April 26, 1987 at age 70.

Larry Barber

Born and reared in central Illinois, Lawrence Barber, who compiled this report, was a newspaper writer for 47 years and continued writing after retiring in 1969. For 37 years he was Marine Editor of the Portland *Oregonian*. During that period he learned of the *Tango* loading at St. Helens. This was in wartime and his published reports were sharply curtailed by Navy censorship. Long after the war he became acquainted with Archie McPhee and Fred Bitte of *Tango*'s crew, and they provided the main portion of this true story of the ship's long sail to South Africa. He is still writing at age 90.

Fred Bitte

One of the older men on the *Tango* was Fred Bitte, the ship's carpenter and donkey engineer. Reared in Rainier, Oregon, he worked on tugs and barges and as a repairman on river vessels in his uncle's floating marine ways in Portland. He worked as a longshoremen loading the *Tango* at St. Helens when he decided to join the ship for the long voyage around Cape Horn. He left the *Tango* in Durban at a doctor's order and returned home to his wife, Margaret, and sons, Larry and Steven. He invested the $6,000 earned on the *Tango* in Oregon timberland. He died May 25, 1987 at age 75.

Gene Luce

Tango's 18-year-old radio operator first saw the Pacific Ocean when, at 16, he hitch-hiked from his home in Bayard, Nebraska, to Astoria, Oregon. He waded into the surf, then spent that night sleeping behind bales of hay in a waterfront building in Astoria. Two years later, Luce was back in Astoria aboard the *Tango*, his home for the next two years. After leaving the ship, he became a licensed radio operator and retired from the sea in 1951. He became a chemical engineer for eastern fruit punch plants. He finally retired at Seagrove, North Carolina, apparently the only surviving crew member of *Tango*'s wartime voyage.